ON OLDER CATS

Second Edition

By

Judith Lindley

Reviewed by J.L. Woodring, DVM.

ISBN 979-8-9891556-0-6 (paperback)

Cover photo Cat: Mary Jane age 12
Owner/Photo: Cassandra Gess
Design by: Pamela Adams

This is a revised and updated edition of On Older Cats originally published 2002 by 1st Books.

Printed in the United States of America

HD
Heartsy's Designs

ACKNOWLEDGEMENT

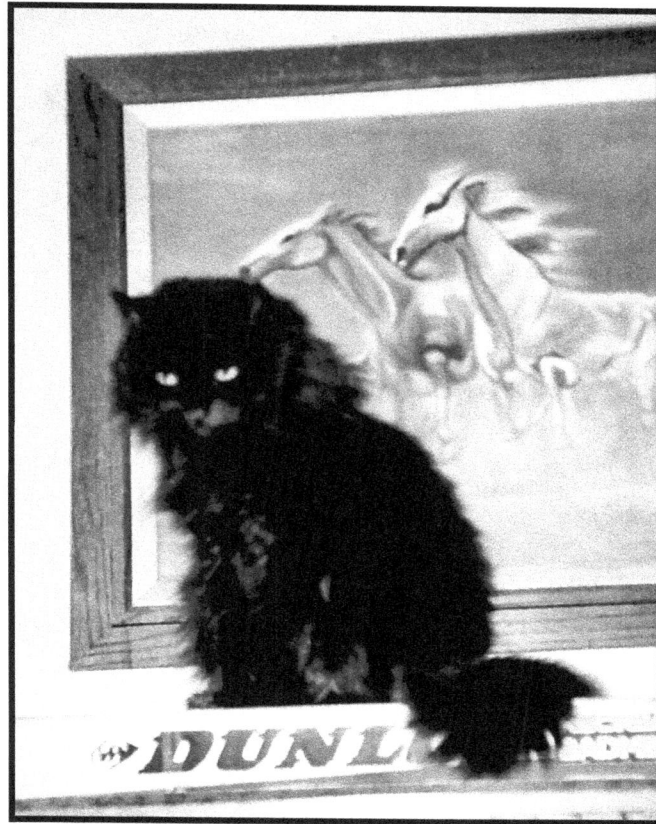

Photo by J. Lindley

I am pleased to acknowledge the help of Elizabeth Mac Innes, of Shelton, Wa., in enabling me to get this information out to web-readers. Her 14 yr. Old cat, Muffy, is presently retired, and living with me, at Animal Helpline's Retirement Home for Cats. (original edition)

I'd like to thank Pamela Adams for her many hours of help with the photos and putting back the text; and her friend, Jaime Rea for her invaluable help with photo enhancements and advice.

- J. Lindley

FRONTISPIECE

WHEN HE STARTS TO SLOW
AND HIS SENSES DIM,
HE'LL NEED TO KNOW
THAT YOU STILL LOVE HIM.

By Judith Lindley (3/19/95)

AUTHOR'S NOTE:

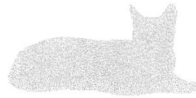

You will find throughout the book that I have referred to the cat in the female gender, as her rather than him. This is because it is easier for me to picture the cat, an animal with such grace, love and endurance, as feminine.

Second Edition

Believe it or not even after more than twenty years the information in these pages is still pretty much the same. I've added a few things to make the reading flow easier and I've changed the drawings. But, all in all, it's not too much different from the original On Older Cats. I hope you will enjoy it.

- Judith Lindley

PREFACE

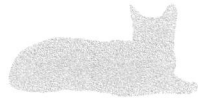

TO THE READER:

This book is not intended to be used as a medical text book. It is intended to provide the everyday cat owner with my observations, coupled with medical relationships when necessary. As the bibliography shows I have carefully researched the medical portions of this book.

While reading this please keep in mind that while 'cats are people too' medically they are not small dogs or small people. Cats are biochemically different and will react differently to medicines used. Always consult with your veterinarian before using any medication on your kitty.

I would like to thank my friend, Jerry Woodring DVM, for his assistance with this venture, insofar as keeping me somewhere in the middle of the road. I would also like to thank my husband, Tom, for putting up with me during the writing. I could not have completed this without either of them. Most of all thank you, the reader, for your interest in older cats.

- Judith Lindley

FOREWORD

It has been quite interesting helping Judith with her book. I have tried very hard to keep her from making any errors in the scientific or medical portions. I have literally worn her out finding source material. I may not totally agree with all of her thoughts but this is her book and her observations are good and will work well for most cat owners and their cats.

I think the cat owners of the world will enjoy her work, especially since it is written in a form that anyone can understand.

- J.L. Woodring, DVM

CONTENTS

INTRODUCTION

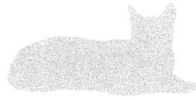

I did not always have a cat. I think though, I must have always had a desire to have one, for as a child I loved the feel of fur. When my mother went to the Broadway, I invariably was found in the fur department, snuggled among the fur coats. The first cat I wanted was a white long haired kitten from next door. She was the only one of the litter who would bound through our hedge to play with me. Unfortunately, my mother had a severe eye blistering allergic reaction, even to me after handling her, so having her was definitely out of the question.

Strangely enough, it was my mother who presented me, at twenty years, with my first litter of kittens. Their mother was injured in a car mishap and was unable to nurse them. They were between seven to ten days old as their eyes were just beginning to open. They seemed to be all mouth and black fur. They had to be bottle fed every three to four hours so I became very attached to them. At the proper intervals they were weaned, litter box trained and all placed but two. I kept a brother and sister not only for my companionship but theirs as well. I've always felt it was easier to have two cats than just one. Now, it seems to be the more the merrier. The two cats, Stokley and Grayless, lived together until Stokley's untimely disappearance at five years old. I still prefer to think of him as being stolen rather than run-over by some misguided black cat hater. Needless to say, Grayless and I went through a period of mourning. The loss was deep but it was made easier by the company of another cat, Miss Kitty, acquired during my second marriage. I knew I could never replace Stokley, each cat is an individual and loved for themselves, but I could love others. Grayless lived to be eighteen and one half years old, aging very gracefully with the exception, her acceptance, of a gradual blindness from fifteen years on.

Grayless lived through, and accepted, all my changes with her gentle kindness and companionship. We graduated from a household of three cats to a cattery rescue situation of one hundred sixty two cats, and back down to a retirement home of sixty plus cats. It's been my good fortune and pleasure to have been able to observe, not only Grayless, but other older cats age gracefully, sometimes well into their twenties. As problems arose I was able to do research to better equip myself to handle whatever they were. It is by writing this book that I hope my observations, and research, will be of some use to others, so more of us can help our beloved feline companions age gracefully.

For many years I have had the opportunity to observe the changes cats go through during their lifespan. I have operated a retirement home, a place for older or handicapped cats, since 1985. I have been privy to many of the subtle changes, as well as the dramatic changes (those due to disease and injury), that they experience. I have learned the importance of veterinary visits and when they are necessary. I've also learned many 'tricks of the trade', things to do to soothe their aging process. Many effects of aging are normal and do not require a veterinary visit, those more dramatic (changes in food and water intake or output) may have an underlying disease and should be checked.

Years ago it was 'put out the cat and go to bed'. Now it's make sure the cat's in before going to bed. Over the last two decades our feline companions have become more important to us. With the advance of science our feline friends are able to live longer lives. Where life expectancy was twelve to fourteen years now it's more like sixteen to eighteen years plus. It is most important for us to be able to recognize the difference between a disease symptom and a normal degenerative condition. We need to know what we can do to make their Golden Years pleasant.

In humans the aging process is emotional as well as physical. So it is true with cats. Their physical deterioration is more noticeable but they also need emotional reassurances that it's OK for them to grow old. They need to know someone cares and will be there for them if they need it.

There are many fine books on cats dealing with general care and physical anatomy. Up until now most of these cat books have dealt with kittens to adult cats, with little, if any, information on older cats. There are changes that specifically affect older cats and we must be ready to recognize them. As with humans, age is partly a state of mind. If your cat has plenty of love, action and attention in her life, chances are really good she will remain your companion for many years.

So… This book is dedicated solely to those special felines, the OLDER CATS.

Photo by J. Lindley

Grayless Aging Gracefully.

CHAPTER I. AGE

Basic biology teaches us that all living matter is made up of units called cells. Within each cell is a nucleus, cytoplasm and DNA, bits of information that determine what the cell will become. The cells multiply, by cellular division, and become groups, which in turn form into tissues and organs needed to for an entire body. Each cell goes through a series of changes, phases, of birth, growth, maturity, reproduction, decline and death. The total of these phases is known as a lifecycle. The time measured to complete the lifecycle is known as a lifespan. This whole process is known as aging. In other words age is the natural progression of time affecting a living body, resulting in a normal decline, breakdown, wearing out and slowing down of body functions ending with death.

Each living thing has a specific lifespan allotted to it. For example an insect may live only a few hours or days, while larger animals live years and decades. The typical lifespan for a mouse is approximately two years, while the normal expected lifespan for a cat is around sixteen years (there are always exceptions). Of course the lifespan of the mouse is definitely altered should the cat decide to eat him. Thus, we have the effects to the normal aging process. These effects, including injuries, diseases and changes in chemical balance, can alter or shorten the lifespan. With advancements in veterinary science we are able to better control these effects and so increase the lifespan of our beloved cats.

Everything in this world ages at a different rate, sometimes we humans can better understand if we compare the particular animal, in this case the cat, to our own ages. These rates are influenced by many things. First is genetic background, or family traits. If your cat is from good healthy stock chances of longevity are very good. Second, physical condition, if maintained with proper diet, timely vaccinations and adequate exercise your pet will be kept free of disease. Third, is the environment. It goes without saying, that the inside cat is much safer than the outside cat. Exposure to the natural elements of extreme heat and cold can be as dangerous as the risks of injuries and disease from encounters with other animals. Fourth, and last, stress plays a most important role, particularly as the cat reaches the older years. Given perfect conditions, the average age expectancy, at this time, is: males 14-16 years; females 16-18 years; alters living anywhere from 2 to 4 years longer in each case. Please remember there are always exceptions to the norm. The use of an age curve along with a Cat Human comparison chart gives a better understanding of our physically and emotionally balanced feline companions. (see Age Curve and Chart)

A young cat matures, reaches expected approximate adult size, around four years old. She will in most cases, appear to be fully grown at one and one half years but she will continue to grow and attain full growth at four years. The emphasis during this growing period is on physical well-being, supplemented with good nutrition and regular vaccinations. Emotionally, the cat is involved with her self, immediate surroundings and relationships with other cats; first mother, then siblings, followed by mating relationships and kitten rearing.

The plateau period, years four to eight, is a stable period. The growing stops and the physical needs become balanced with the emotional needs. The cat now relates more to other cats in her own peer group. The cat will tend to be a homebody and prefer to 'rule the roost' over any younger cats. Required nutrition becomes a maintenance diet. Health problems are at a minimum but vaccinations are still advisable particularly if in close contact with other cats.

Age Curve

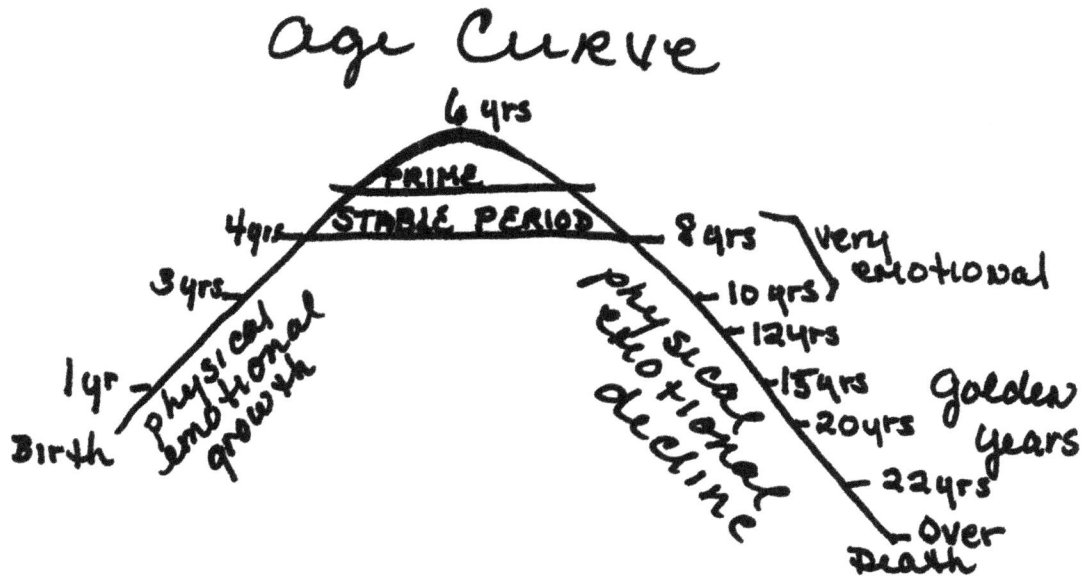

CAT - HUMAN COMPARISON CHART

CAT	HUMAN
Birth to 4 yrs	Birth to 25 yrs
4 yrs to 8 yrs	25 yrs to 40 yrs
8 yrs to 10 yrs	40 yrs to 50 yrs
10 yrs to 12 yrs	50 yrs to 60 yrs
12 yrs to 15 yrs	60 yrs to 70 yrs
15 yrs to 20 yrs	70 yrs to 90 yrs
20 yrs to 22 yrs+	90 yrs to 100 yrs+

Charts figured by own observations - J. Lindley

There is a gentle decline between the ages of eight to ten. Cats are very emotionally touchy during this period. Cats of this age are comparable to humans of forty to fifty years, a time of mid-life crises. They can be very closely bonded with their humans and any extreme changes can be very traumatizing for them. This would be a bad time to cause the cat to become separated, as she may will herself dead. During this age period the cat will prefer the feline company of younger cats and kittens. It is as if she realizes that she's growing older but needs to prove that she's still young and active and has many years still ahead.

The next decline is seen around ten to twelve years and will pretty much extend through the fourteenth year. The cat will now favor the company of older adult cats, particularly those over fifteen years. You may notice your cat becoming a 'nurse cat' or caregiver. She will enjoy washing the older ones. Around twelve years the cat should become more emotionally stable and it is a good time to visit the veterinarian for a routine examination. He should be able to tell you what type of health problems to watch for based on the general appearance of your cat. Around twelve years old your cat needs to be shifted to an adult diet. Your veterinarian can recommend one based on your cat's weight and potential health problems. A higher quality food may be more expensive but in the long run you will save money on veterinarian visits.

Just passed fifteen years old you will notice more decline in your cat. Although all the body organs slow down at a different rate now is when more changes will occur. The organs will tend to lose their natural moisture, which will hasten their normal breakdown. Your cat may begin to slowly lose weight. It seems, in most cases, the older they get the thinner they become. Most important, anytime your cat goes off her feed or appears just not right watch for signs of dehydration. Pay particular attention to water intake as many diseases can show up at this time. Emotions are again volatile and your cat may go through a period of being crabby. She may also become a finicky eater. Finicky eating is usually attributed to various health reasons but, sometimes the cat is actually just seeking more attention from you. For much of her life, to this point, your cat has devoted most of her emotional attention toward you. You have been the controller of her world, her god, the one most adored and pretty much the center of her whole life. Your cat will suddenly realize that, due to her advancing age, she can no longer watch over you properly. In some cases, she will reject this and seem to be bewildered. Your cat will seek more and more attention. I believe old cats are looking for reassurance that it's all right for them to grow old and that you still love them in spite of their infirmities. Their eye sight may be dimming, their hearing fading and they just aren't quite fast enough to catch that mouse any longer. Arthritis may set in which only adds to their frustration. They may wait for you to help them to their favorite perch, rather than risk a fall, especially if they've already missed once.

If your cat does fall, a pulled muscle, or worse, damaged internal organs, can be very painful. Cats bear their pain with a quiet dignity so sometimes it's hard for us to notice any discomfort. Rather than rushing to the veterinarian, when you do notice something, it is wiser to phone first. Unnecessary trips, particularly to the veterinarian, can cause stress-trauma which can be more harmful to your cat than what is ailing her. Your veterinarian should be able to tell you, based on health history, whether it's something to be concerned about and may be able to give you the necessary advice, right over the phone.

Normal degeneration of organs with age cannot be stopped, but pain and discomfort, in most cases, can be alleviated. Of course, if you notice any unusual lumps, at any age, your cat should be seen immediately. Tumors, if observed and removed soon enough, should not become cancerous. Cancer can be a big problem in older cats, but if treated soon; your cat can survive it. One must remember that in any surgery the anesthesia risk is very great for an older cat, so only life threatening problems should be treated by surgery. Expect the recovery/recuperative time to be slower, at least twenty- four hours more for every five years of age.[1]

Our feline companions may have been through our emotional strife of growing up, or perhaps they've just been the silent companion we've cried on. Now we need to be there for them. By becoming more aware of what to expect as their years go by we can help them enjoy their Golden Years.

NOTE

[1] *Michael S. Bodri, "Care of Older Animals, Life Span and Aging." Animal Science, Study Unit 11 Animal Care: Prenatal Through Old Age (Scranton, P.A: ICS Intangibles Holding Co. 1990): 43*

CHAPTER II OUTWARD CHANGES

The first things noticed with age are seen as outward, or external, changes. Eventually all changes, internal organ breakdown included, are seen on the outside, either by sign or by action. The sensory organs, eyes, ears, nose and mouth, usually, exhibit the earliest signs. These will be followed by skin and coat changes. Finally an overall slump to the body exhibited as changes in paws, claws and posture. There will be an audible change as well, the interrupted purr. Your cat will rely on you to recognize these changes to determine what natural breakdown is and what may need medical attention.

1. EYES

The first thing you'll notice about your cat, when she comes to you, will be those beautiful mystic eyes. If in fact, the eyes are the windows to the soul then cats must have a truly beautiful soul. In relation to other animals, the cat has the biggest eyes in proportion to its body weight.[1] It would have been more appropriate if it had been a cat to whom Red Riding Hood spoke when she said, "What big eyes you have, Grandma!" for they surely are "All the better to see you with." In fact, although they cannot see in total darkness, they can see six times better, in the dark, than humans do.[2] Cats also see in a wider spectrum than humans. They are able to see ultra violet rays and other light sources normally invisible to humans.[3] A cat is a predator so the eyes are placed up front. Due to the placement of their eyes cats have a wider range,

11

up to 280 degrees, of vision, however, they have less three dimensional perspective, than humans.[4] Strangely, also because of eye placement, in relation to their nose, I've noticed cats cannot see immediately under their nose. All this adds up to make the feline eyes truly the most fascinating eyes of the entire Animal Kingdom.

The eyes, of the cat, are very complex organs with many parts, fluids, connecting muscles and glands. The major parts of the eye are the cornea, aqueous and vitreous fluids, iris, pupil, lens, retina, tapetum lucidum and the optic nerve. The white part of the eye, usually barely visible, the sclera is not directly affected by aging but may reflect other bodily age related problems. The tear duct, upper and lower eyelids, the third eyelid (the haw, attached to the lower eyelid at the nose corner) and the conjunctiva (lining of the eyelids) are also effected by age and will be discussed later.

Not all parts of the eyes are affected by age but the ones that are are definitely major parts. The iris, lens, retina, tapetum lucidum, tear duct, cornea, the aqueous and vitreous fluids are all affected to some extent. Even the eyeball will appear smaller. The eyeball, itself, may lose an immeasurable amount of fluids, but this smaller appearance is due mostly to fluid loss in the surrounding tissues. The eyes appear to sink in.[5] This sink-eye happens in the most advanced years and can possibly be related to dehydration from chronic renal failure, also accompanying old age. Earlier signs are much more subtle.

The cornea is a clear protective layer on the front of the eye. The aqueous fluid is lubricating fluid, lying in a chamber, beneath the cornea. Moving inward, the iris is the colored area you see. The iris adjusts, the amount of light entering, by opening (dilating) or closing (constricting). The black hole, or slit, you see is the pupil, the opening in the iris. Behind the pupil is the lens, a clear structure that focuses the light onto the back lining, the retina. The tapetum lucidum lines the retina. The vitreous fluid is in the larger chamber of the eyeball between the lens and the retina. The optic nerve is attached to the back of the eye.

The sleeping cat awakes, lifts her head and slowly blinks her eyes. The light passes into the cornea and is directed toward the center of the iris. Immediately the iris adjusts the amount of light received. The light passes through the pupil and onto the lens where the light is focused, as it passes through, and shines on the retina. Special cells, lying with the retina, distinguish the shape and shades of the light. Chemical changes within these cells trigger a message, a visual impulse, which is sent to the brain, through the optic nerve, where they are recognized as an object. If she happens to looking at you, look back and check her eyes. If the third eyelid is covering her eye, or eyes, it may mean she isn't feeling too well.

On a close inspection of the iris, the colored area, you will notice small lines, sometimes squiggles, of dark coloration. In the blue eyes the color will be a dark blue-gray, in green and gold eyes the color will be a dark brown. In amber and dark eyes it's just a darker squiggle. You may also see bluish areas in green eyes. These colors are changes in pigmentation and subtly begin somewhere around twelve years old. There may be brown or orange flecks in the iris as well. These flecks or freckles are normal and may be in younger cat's eyes as well. The flecks may increase in number and size with advancing years. These color changes are harmless and will not obstruct normal vision.[6] The next change occurs around fifteen years or more. This change is seen as a slight opacity, or haze, in the pupil, the black area of the eye. The pupil, itself, is an opening and is not actually affected. What you are seeing is the lens of the eye. The lens grows slowly, with new cells forming, throughout the cat's life. (The lens does not increase in size, once full size is reached, but cells die and are replaced continuously within the actual limited size.) As the new fibrous cells are formed in the center, the older ones are pushed toward the edges. This causes the center to be more dense than the edges. The entire lens loses water, as it ages, adding to the density, causing it to become hardened. This overall change, of the lens causes a grayish appearance, visible, to us, through the pupil. Although this condition is part of the normal aging process, it does have a clinical name, nuclear sclerosis (nuclear for center and sclerosis for hardening). Nuclear sclerosis (also known as lenticular sclerosis) does not appreciably obstruct vision, although, it may be accompanied, in advanced years, by cataracts, particularly senile cataracts.[7]

The retina is the part of the eye made up of special cells called rods and cones. These are sensors which convert the light, entering the pupil, passing through the lens, into nerve impulses. The nerve impulses are carried, to the brain's visual center, to determine colors and shapes. The human eye has more cones, than rods, enabling us to see distinct colors. The cat's eye, adapted more for night vision, has more rods, enabling them to see more distinctly the shades of black and white.[8] Cats, having cones, are able to see somewhat in color, but their use of night vision is much more important to them, for many still do their best mousing at night. There can be a retinal degeneration caused by nutritional deficiency, specifically of taurine, which leads to eventual blindness in the older cat.[9] Once the deficiency has been supplemented the progression of degeneration should stop. In some of my older cats, particularly the ones with blue eyes, I've noticed sensitivity to direct light. Fortunately for the cat, and only the Felis class,[10] their slit pupil helps. The slit pupil is able to close tighter, than the rounded pupil, to allow more protection to sensitive eyes.

Lying beneath the retina is the tapetum lucidum. The tapetum lucidum is made up of specialized reflective cells, located mostly on the upper half of the eye. Its function is to reflect any light not absorbed, during the first passage through the retina, back for a second time to be absorbed. This is the action, during night vision that enables the cat to see so well in semi-darkness. This is also what you see, when light bounces off the cat's eyes, in the dark. With age there may be a slow breakdown of these cells which may contribute to the light sensitivity, discussed previously. This natural breakdown can be seen as a change in reflected color. A normal color, in a younger cat, is silver-gold. In an older one it will be a deeper burnt gold. In cat's eyes that reflect red the color appears more of a burnt orange.[11]

Lastly, the sclera, is the covering of the eye, to which the cornea is attached, as a window on the front. The sclera, itself, is not normally affected by age but is a mirror for other possible health problems. For example, in the case of failing liver or kidneys, the sclera will be a yellow color, indicating a buildup of system impurities. In the event of trauma, or injury, to the head, the sclera may have a reddish-brown color in the top corner, indicating damage done to small blood vessels.

The tear duct, also affected by age, will water or have a discharge. The discharge, a weeping, should be normally clear and may build up a mild crust. This discharge is an early symptom of sinus breakdown, normally occurring with age.[12] The older the cat, the more discharge. A damp cloth, or tissue, may be used to gently clean the area. Be tender, your baby is old and may object to this. If the discharge leaves a red irritated area you may wish to ask your veterinarian about an antibiotic ointment.

Allergies seem to be more common with age. Your older cat's eyes will be more sensitive to pollen and dust.[13] The eyes will appear red and watery. Due to this sensitivity the eye is subject to bacterial infections of the conjunctiva, the lining of the inner eyelids. This is called conjunctivitis and it causes an increased mattering which usually requires antibiotics.

There are diseases, or conditions, specifically associated with certain parts of the eye, attributed to age. They can be seen in middle-aged, as well as older, cats. The most common diseases are corneal necrosis, cataracts and glaucoma, which can also be called a condition.

Corneal necrosis, also called corneal sequestrum, is a buildup of plaque on the cornea of the cat's eye. It may be associated with a weakened, or poorly, functioning tear duct. If the eye is not kept moist, by blinking and proper tearing it will dry out. (Even though cats seem to stare for hours they do eventually blink.) The plaque buildup looks like the brown freckles but will grow larger and will often be accompanied by a dark tearing. This may be very painful to your cat, and she will rub or wash her eye a lot. Early management may include applications of artificial tears and antibiotics. A bad buildup will require surgical removal. As surgery is a risk for an older cat the sooner you notice any unusual change the better.

Cataracts can be easily confused with nuclear sclerosis as they both cause the lens to become opaque. Cataracts may even accompany nuclear sclerosis in the aging cat. When your veterinarian peers into your cat's eye he will receive a normal visual response with nuclear sclerosis, but no response is apparent if a cataract is obstructing the vision. What causes cataracts, particularly senile cataracts, is not altogether known at this time. Some cats seem to be more predisposed to developing cataracts than others. Since cataracts can be removed, 'sucked out' so to speak, it is possible that they are caused by an irritant, or the eye's response to an irritant.[14] Fortunately normal senile cataracts progress slowly, and the cat can adapt to any visual impairment. There is, unfortunately, a bad side to this. The onset of cataracts can also be an indication of diabetes, so you may wish to have your cat examined and checked when cataracts are noticed. The best news is that feline cataracts are not as common as canine cataracts. And, even though your cat is getting older she may not have them at all.

While corneal necrosis and cataracts mimic, to some extent, the natural aging processes, glaucoma is a condition completely unto itself. It is the result of a malfunction which causes a fluid buildup in the aqueous humor, the fluid between the cornea and the lens. It may appear in only one eye. Signs to look for include reddening of the eye, cloudy cornea, changes in color of the iris and fixed dilated pupil. The cat will usually display excessive rubbing and blinking.

In the 1980s the slow blink became popular. It was deemed that it was the cat's way of saying I Love You. You could return it by slow blinking back. Regular blinking is fine but any abnormal rubbing, washing, blinking or tearing should require a trip to the veterinarian. Early treatment is mandatory to protect those most precious mystic eyes. In the case of the cat's eye, beauty is not in the eye of the beholder - but in the eye of the beheld.

Trisket, a 15 year old, is a stunning example of "older" eyes. She lives with Martha Nishitani in Seattle, Washington.

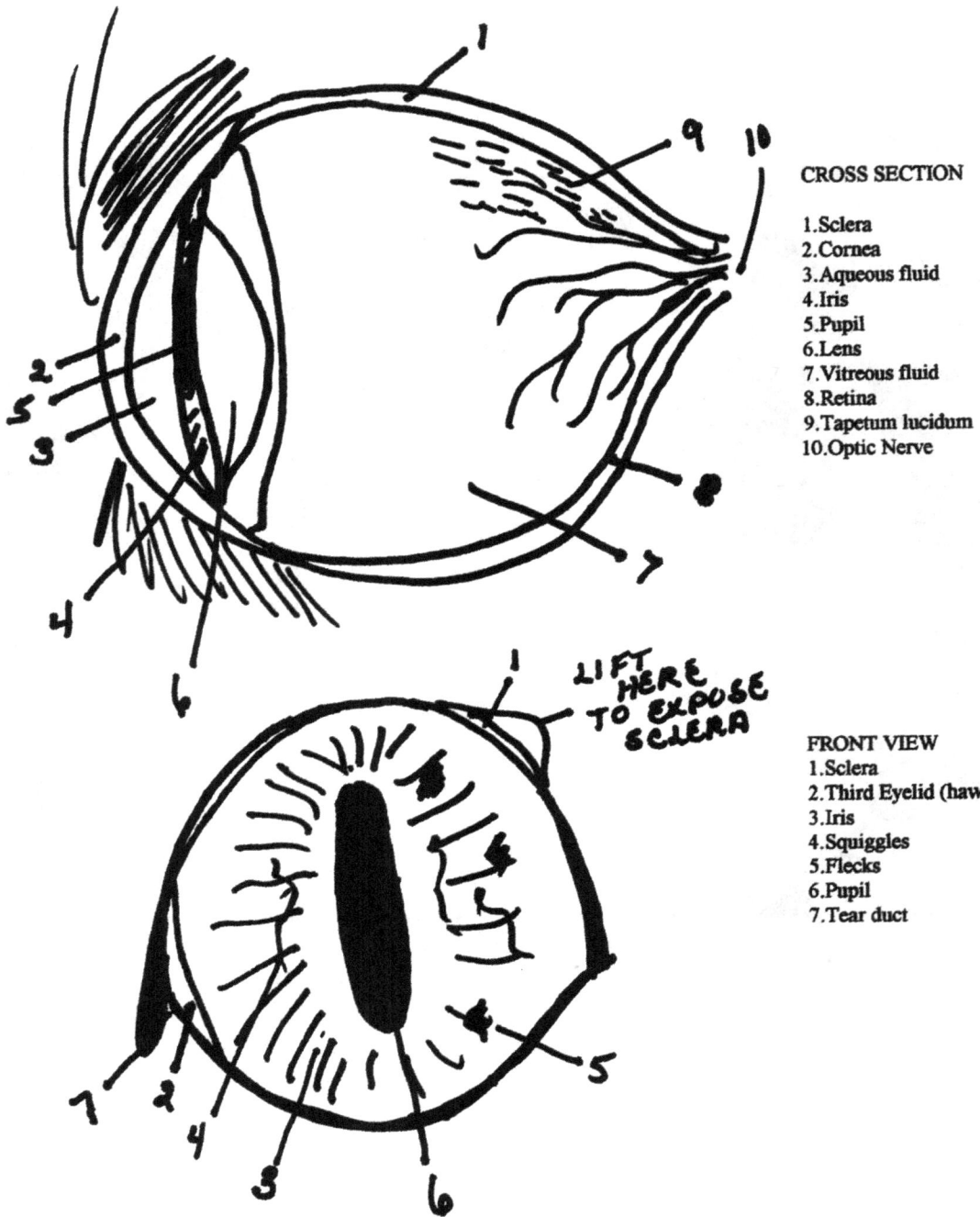

CROSS SECTION

1. Sclera
2. Cornea
3. Aqueous fluid
4. Iris
5. Pupil
6. Lens
7. Vitreous fluid
8. Retina
9. Tapetum lucidum
10. Optic Nerve

LIFT HERE TO EXPOSE SCLERA

FRONT VIEW

1. Sclera
2. Third Eyelid (haw)
3. Iris
4. Squiggles
5. Flecks
6. Pupil
7. Tear duct

THE CAT'S EYE

18

NOTES

1 *Fernand Mery, et al. The Life History and Magic of the Cat (New York: Madison Square Press, 1968): 124.*

2 *Jeffrey E. Barlough, Linda Susan Jorgensen and Ronald C. Riis, Sensory Organs and Disorders, The Cornell Book of Cats (New York: Villard Books, div. of Random House, 1992): 167.*

3 *Fernand Mery, et al. The Life History and Magic of the Cat (New York: Madison Square Press, 1968): 123.*

4 *Same as 1 cited above.*

5 *Personal observations, J. Lindley.*

6 *Jeffrey E. Barlough, Linda Susan Jorgensen and Ronald C Riis, Sensory Organs and Disorders, The Cornell Book of Cats (New York: Villard Books, div. of Random House, 1992): 173.*

7 *Same as 2. cited previously.*

8 *Reader's Digest Illustrated Book of Cats (N.Y. Reader's Digest, 1992): 54 & 156.*

9 *Margaret Reister, "Good Nutrition Shines Through," Cat Fancy Magazine (May 1995): 10.*

10 *Animal Health Newsletter, Cornell University (June 1987) Questions and Answers.*

11 *Personal observation, J. Lindley.*

12 *Personal observation, J. Lindley.*

13 *Personal observation, J. Lindley.*

14 *Personal opinion, drawn from information by Jeffrey E. Barlough, Linda Susan Jorgensen and Ronald C. Riis, Sensory Organs and Disorders, The Cornell Book of Cats (N.Y.: Villard Books div of Random House, 1992): 172.*

2. EARS

Cat's ears come in all sizes and shapes as befits their particular breed of cat. Some are very extreme and pointy (Siamese), some smaller, rounded and very furry (Persian) and some very large with practically no fur at all (Sphynx). Then there are the beautiful anomalies, from mutated genes, those that fold (Scottish Fold) and curl (American Curl). Of course, there are mixtures of all these styles but whatever their shape; cat's ears are truly magnificent structures. In peak working conditions the cat's ears can pick up to 65,000 hertz (cycles per second), which is much higher than humans at 20,000 hertz.[1] This not only allows cats to hear the soft nibbling of a mouse, in the far reaches of your house, but may also enable them to determine what's being eaten.

Anatomically, the ear can be divided into three main parts: the outer ear; the middle ear; and the inner ear. The outer ear includes the pinna, canal and ear drum. The pinna is an envelope like structure supported by cartilage and supplied by many small muscles. These small muscles work together to move the ear in the direction of the sound waves. The primary function of the pinna is to collect and funnel the sound waves down into the canal. The canal is a dark tube, or passageway, for the sound waves, ending at the ear drum (tympanic membrane). The ear drum acquires the sound waves and intensifies them, through vibrations, then passes them on to the middle ear.

The middle ear contains small bones, ossicles, through which the sound waves are passed and transformed into a purer state for the inner ear. Also connected to the middle ear is the eustachian tube, a passage to the back of the throat. The eustachian tube aids in equalizing pressure by passing air, coming in through the mouth, to the ear drum, causing it to "pop".[2] This is much like humans popping their ears as they change elevations. Being closely associated with the back of the throat, during extreme upper respiratory (sinus) infections there may be drainage, from the sinus cavities, passing through the throat into the eustachian tube. This drainage is a rather miserable condition for the cat.

Passing through the middle ear the sound waves reach the inner ear. The inner ear is made up of the vestibular system and the shell like cochlea. The vestibular system is a set of fluid filled canals, semi circular canals. These canals control the balance and the body position of the cat. The cochlea contains the Organ of Corti, the hearing organ. The sound waves coming into the cochlea are converted into electrical impulses. The impulses are carried by the auditory nerve to the cat's brain.

The tissues of the ear structures are like all other organs of the cat's body. With age they lose some of their natural moisture. Depending on the structure involved the cat may be affected in two ways, balance disturbances or diminished hearing. Results of these changes should become apparent as the cat approaches fifteen years. Balance disturbances may show up before a noticeable hearing loss. Sometimes as early as ten years, you may notice your cat just doesn't climb as many trees or prefers the floor more to the counter. Normally, the older cat is able to adjust to balance problems on a daily basis. However, the more advanced the age the more carefully she'll move around. If startled, she may even stagger or fall. Then, embarrassed, she'll look around to see if anyone saw her. If falling becomes a problem, your cat may wait to be lifted.

The older cat is able to disguise her deafness from you, especially if there are younger cats around, by watching more intently what's happening around her. She can appear at meal-times and act like she hears the can opener, just like all the others. Since older cats tend to sleep more deeply they can be easily startled, even if they're mildly deaf. The one way to really tell if she's deaf is to call her by name and check the response. Cats can live into their twenties without a significant hearing loss.

The tissues of the outer ear flap, the pinna, become more delicate with age. The scourge of cat's ears is the dreaded ear mite. The ear mite is a small bug, a parasite, whose favorite place of abode is in the warm, dark ear canal. As the mite moves around inside it causes the cat great discomfort. Ear mites leave a very tell-tale sign, a dirty sludge, visible to the human eye, on the ear flap and in the vertical portion of the ear canal. The ear mite, itself is invisible and can only be seen with a microscope. If you notice the problem soon enough a mitacide can be purchased and applied to eliminate the mites before any real damage can be done. Although the mites live in the ear canal the most severe damage is done to the ear flap tissue. In bad infestations, the cat will violently shake her head and scratch at her ears, trying to get the darned bug out. Other infections very rarely cause this intense itching. An older cat can seriously damage her ear flap by shaking too violently. The result is a hematoma, a buildup of blood retained in the envelope of the flap. In some cases the blood may be drained by a veterinarian, in others it's reabsorbed. In either event, the cat may be left with a withered or permanently folded ear. This can happen in cats of any age but more so with older cats, due to the tender ear tissue.

Exposure to the sun, over a long period of time, can also be damaging to the delicate aging ear flap tissue. Cats with light color ear skin, particularly white ears, are especially sensitive. Extreme cases of sunburn (solar dermatitis) can result in a form of skin cancer, squamous cell cancer.[3] Early signs are red blistered areas that won't heal. In advanced cases the ear flaps may be trimmed to remove the cancerous areas.

Another form of possible cancer, associated with middle-aged and older cats, is a ceruminous gland tumor. This is a tumor of the ceruminous gland, the wax producing gland, in the ear canal. They are dark cyst-like growths appearing anywhere from the edges to the depths of the ear canal, and may even penetrate the ear drum. They may either be benign (non-cancerous) or malignant (cancerous), and be subject to removal. Surgical removal depends on the size and location of the tumor.[4] Again, as in any surgery, the risk factor, due to stress and age, must be seriously considered. Consult your veterinarian.

Position of the ears is very important for health reasons as well as communications. Younger cats, being naturally inquisitive, move their ears in all directions, so as not to miss anything happening around them. Middle-aged and older cats seem to have only two main ear positions, the Frontal and what I call the Leave-Me-Alone positions. The Frontal position is a normal relaxed position. It tells you everything is fine with the cat, at that moment. This position also allows you to quickly scan the ear opening for any dirty waxy buildup that may indicate a problem.

The Leave-Me-Alone position is a signal that the cat wants its own space. Your cat will hold her ears in a flattened down position. This flat position is not quite as flat as in an angry cat. It takes a lot to make an older cat angry, so extremely flat is something you won't see often, if at all. The Leave-Me-Alone position is used when another cat approaches too closely or if the cat's supper is in jeopardy. If you notice one ear held differently than the other, be sure to look inside. There is usually a definite reason for this position which could be of health concern.

The gift of hearing is as precious to animals as it is to humans and we must help them to protect it while they have it. Ear infections are almost always accompanied by a rather pungent odor. This odor should be noticeable whether you poke your nose in or not. Your daily observance of them will tell you if there are any unusual problems. Cats spend a lot of time washing their face and cleaning their ears but somehow their paws just don't quite fit inside, so they must rely on us for help.

Whether they're folded, curled, straight or rounded, no matter what their position, the cat's ears are unique and impressive auditory structures.

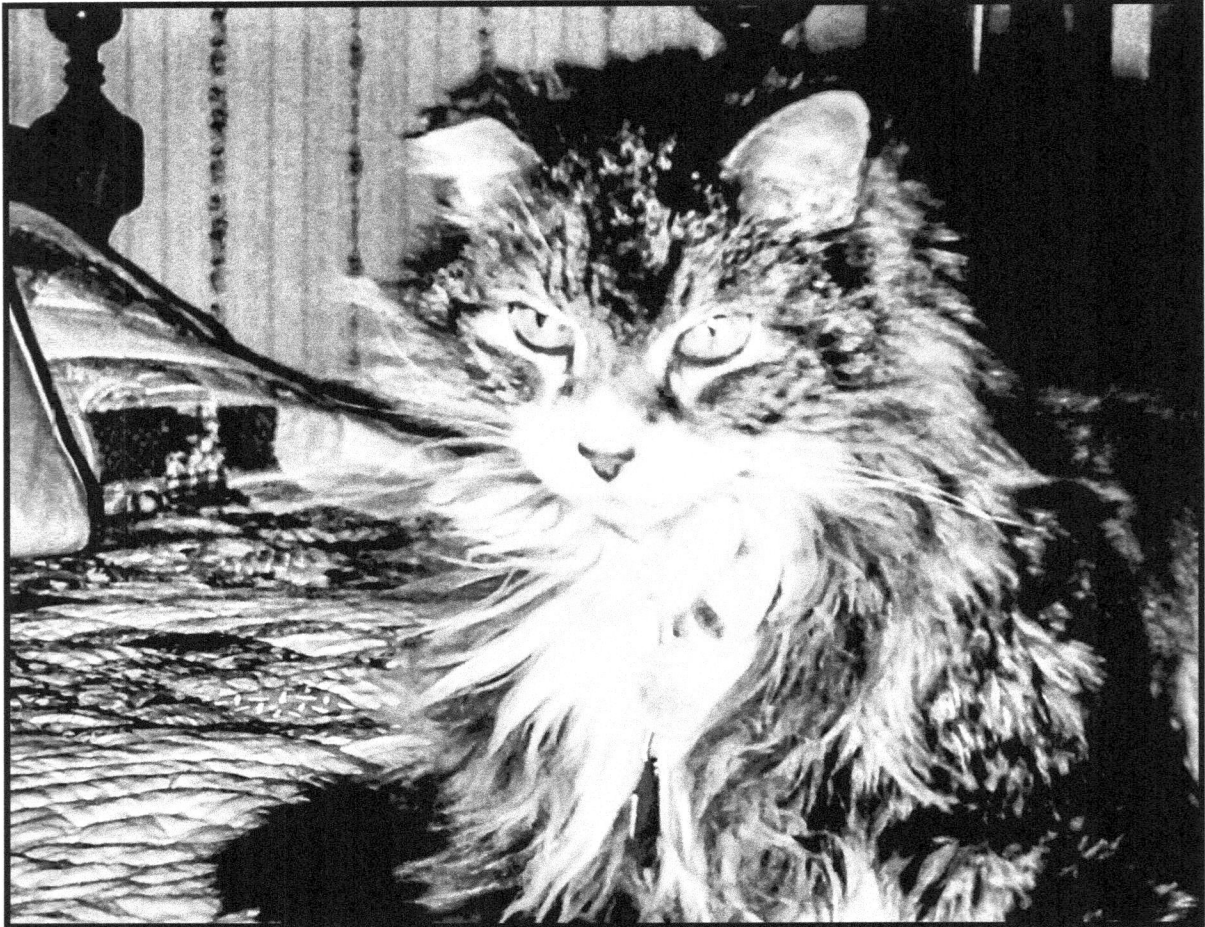

Tinker, at the grand old age of 19 years, is a good example of surviving ear problems. He lives with Barbara Aring in Cleveland, Ohio.

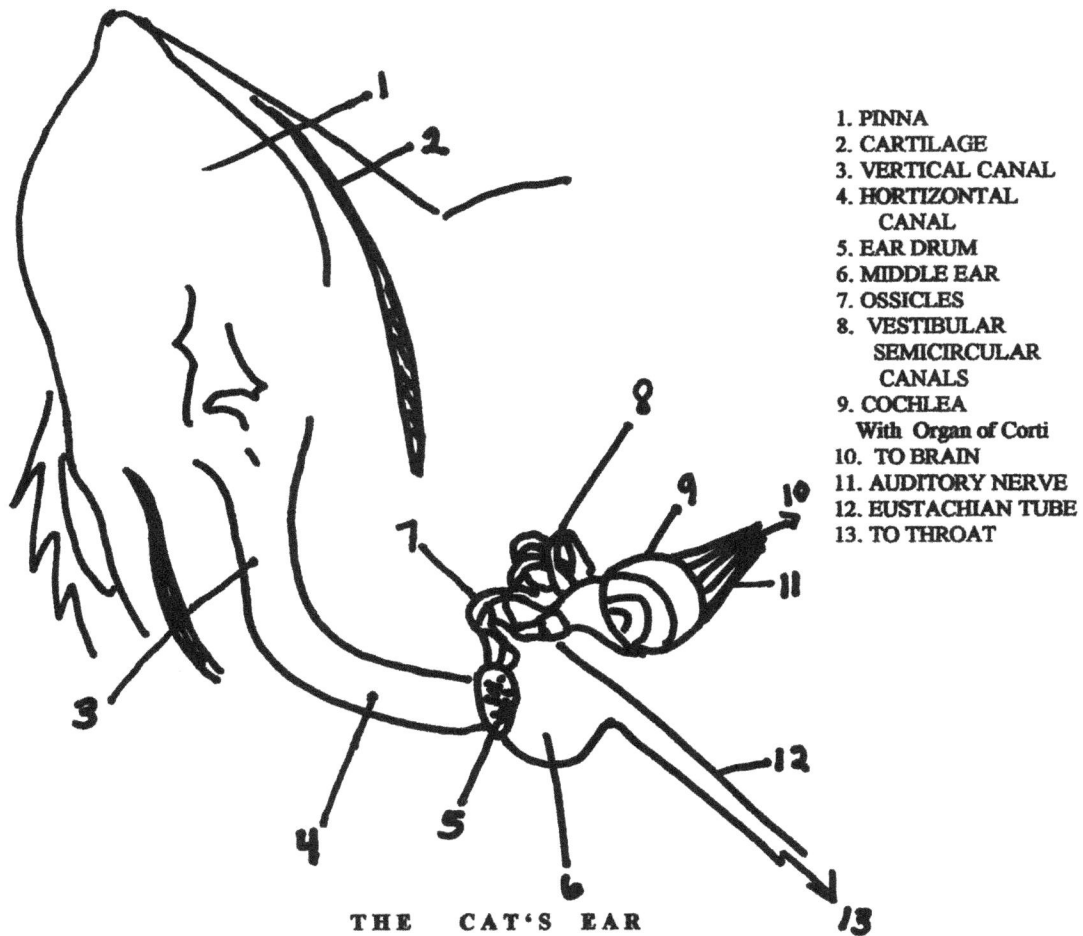

1. PINNA
2. CARTILAGE
3. VERTICAL CANAL
4. HORTIZONTAL CANAL
5. EAR DRUM
6. MIDDLE EAR
7. OSSICLES
8. VESTIBULAR SEMICIRCULAR CANALS
9. COCHLEA With Organ of Corti
10. TO BRAIN
11. AUDITORY NERVE
12. EUSTACHIAN TUBE
13. TO THROAT

THE CAT'S EAR

NOTES

1 *Catnip, Newsletter of Tufts University School of Veterinary Medicine (June 1994): 1.*

2 *Jeffrey E. Barlough, Linda Susan Jorgensen and Ronald C. Riis, Sensory Organs and Disorders, The Cornell Book of Cats, (N.Y.: Villard Books, div. of Random House, 1992): 175.*

3 *Catnip, Newsletter of Tufts University School of Veterinary Medicine (June 1994): 1.*

4 *Jeffrey E. Barlough, Linda Susan Jorgensen and Ronald C. Riis, Sensory Organs and Disorders, The Cornell Book of Cats, (N.Y.: Villard Books, div. of Random House, 1992): 176.*

3. NOSE

'The nose knows', or so it goes. Like the eyes and ears the nose also comes in a variety of colors and shapes as befits the breed of cat. They come in hues of pink, beige, rose, rust, brown, gray and black. They can be solid colored, speckled, edged or two colored. The facial structure of the nose can be extremely long and straight (Siamese) to the snub, broad nose (Persian) and all varieties in between.

The structure of the nose is almost as fascinating as its many colors. The twitchy nose leather is known as the planum nasal. The split, eventually separating the lips, is the philtrum.[1] The nostrils, nares, lead into the nasal cavity. Above and connected to the nasal cavity are open spaces in the bones called sinuses. The nasal cavity is divided into two passages, one from each nare, that open at the throat behind the soft palate. The separating cartilage is called the septum. Inside the nasal cavity are bony plates called turbinates. The turbinates are covered with a spongy membrane, the mucosa, which contains the hair-like receptors, the olfactory cells. Also contained within the nasal cavity are serous and mucous glands.

The operations of the nose are very interesting. Odor particles, sniffed by the cat, enter the nares and pass into the nasal cavity. The particles are caught by the receptors and dissolved in moisture, secreted by the glands. The receptors are nerve cells which interpret the smell and forward the signal to the olfactory bulb, or lobe, in the brain for determination of the smell. Exactly how the odor particle is interpreted to a specific smell is still pretty much a mystery. It is thought that the more pungent an odor, the more stimulation of the receptor and stronger the signal. Each smell is categorized in order of strength of odor. The nose has two other normal functions, besides smell, that keep the cat healthy. It filters and warms the incoming air. Particles that might be dangerous to the cat are filtered by small hairs, the mucociliary blanket, which moves sticky mucus, a fluid secreted by the mucous gland, toward the throat and the nares. Bacteria and foreign bodies are passed back out of the nose through this mucus, in example sniffles or sneezing. The mucous and serous glands also produce liquids that help keep the nasal cavity warm and moist. This warms the incoming air so it is healthier for the cat's warm body.

As the cat ages dehydration, moisture lost, becomes a problem for the nose. Dehydration causes the mucociliary blanket to slow down, which causes the mucus layer to thicken and become ineffective. This ineffectiveness allows foreign bodies to enter more readily. The foreign bodies may be anything from simple allergens to fatal viral and bacterial infections.

With age, the tissues in the sinus cavities become easily irritated and allergies become more of a problem. An allergy is the normal response of the nasal system to remove a foreign body. The response is a release of liquid from either the serous gland or the mucous gland. A normal allergic reaction will have clear liquid. A response to a bacterial or viral infection will produce cloudy or milky fluid. Either way the result of this reaction is the inevitable sneeze.

There are two nasal inflammations common to middle-aged and older cats. Rhinitis, inflammation of the mucous membranes, the mucosa, causes a watery discharge. Sinusitis, inflammation of the sinus membranes, causes a thicker milky-white or yellow discharge. Your veterinarian can determine which it is and prescribe either an antihistamine or an antibiotic. Remember, with age, the nasal tissues become tender and it is best they be checked to avoid a chronic problem.

Chronic nasal (respiratory tract) infections can result in polyps. Polyps are a pendulous growth, usually benign, which begin as an enlargement of one of the mucous glands.[2] Indications of the presence of polyps are noisy breathing, nasal discharge and occasional sneezing. There are other forms of cancers and tumors that may even result in facial deformities, but they are fairly uncommon in cats.[3] Only polyps or tumors that interfere with the natural breathing, or swallowing, process should be surgically removed. A facial sore may look ugly to us but the cat may not notice it at all.

The cat uses her nose for a multitude of things. Sniffing is an important part of communication. When a cat meets another cat, especially if it's one she knows but hasn't seen for a while, they will sniff noses then sniff rears. This tells the cat not only who it is but where they've been and what they've been up to. In the case of a female in heat, the male will sniff the female prior to mating with her. If the male particularly likes an odor he will sniff not only with his nose but also with a special organ in the roof of his mouth, the Jacobson's organ.[4] He will open his mouth slightly, curling his lip, while sniffing to enhance the odor being enjoyed. This action is known as the flehmen response, or flehmening. Unfortunately, with the good comes the bad. Dangerous viruses, such as feline infectious peritonitis and feline viral leukemia, can also infect cats through the nose.[5] Most of the inhalant diseases are covered by vaccinations and usually affect younger cats. The older ones are at risk because of their failing immune systems. So, the older cat, if allowed outside, should be current on all vaccinations.

A degenerative condition, sinus breakdown, begins around fourteen years and older.[6] In purebreds, particularly those with severe noses, such as the Siamese or Persians, sinus breakdown may begin slightly earlier. A slight sniffle is the first indication. The older the cat gets the more severe the nasal discharge may become. Around sixteen or seventeen years, if the cat is displaying sinus breakdown, your cat will begin intermittent sneezing and have a chronic runny nose. The danger with this natural aging process is that the cat's nose can also become clogged up and further diminish her ability to smell. The cat will lose her interest in food and her appetite will decrease. Regular cleaning of the nose will prevent much of this problem. Use a damp cloth, or paper towel, as the nose pad will be sensitive. If the nose pad becomes dry and crusty you may apply a small amount of Vaseline® to soothe it. There are vitamin supplements (my favorite is Nutrical®) that may be given to build up your cat and increase her appetite.

In peak working condition the cat's nose is able to smell four times better than the average human's nose.[7] This is because the cat's nose has a greater number of scent-analyzing cells than humans. To be more precise, 67 million cat's to between 5 and 20 million humans.[8] Even with her sense of smell diminishing with age, an older cat can still out smell her owner. So, the next time you think her litter box stinks, imagine what your cat thinks. The nose, or at least her nose, really does know after all.

Photo by J. Lindley

This nose belongs to Callie, age 19, of Animal Helpline.

1. **NOSE LEATHER**
   (Planum Nasal)

2. **NARE**

3. **PHILTRUM**

4. **SINUSES**

5. **NASAL CAVITY**

6. **TURBINATES**

7. **JACOBSON'S ORGAN**

THE CAT'S NOSE

NOTES

[1] *Thomas G. Morrisey, "Catanatomy", Cornell Feline Health Center's Perspectives On Cats, (Summer 1990): 4.*

[2] *Fred W. Scott, Respiratory System and Disorders, The Cornell Book of Cats (N.Y.: Villard Books, div of Random House 1992): 223.*

[3] *ibid.*

[4] *Same as 1 cited.*

[5] *Amy Shojai, "The Sensitive Nose", Cat Fancy Magazine (May 1994): 24.*

[6] *Personal observations - J. Lindley.*

[7] *Dennis Kelsey-Wood, The Atlas of Cats of the World, (New Jersey: T.F.H. 1989): 87.*

[8] *Amy Shojai, "The Sensitive Nose", Cat Fancy Magazine (May 1994): 22.*

4. WHISKERS

I once thought whiskers came only in colors of black and white but on looking at my sixteen year old gray longhair, Princess, I found she had gray whiskers with only a few white ones. This got me curious. On close inspection of two chocolate point Siamese, Grandpa seventeen and Minou nine, I found not only solid white whiskers but white with brown flecks. The younger, Minou, had mostly the two colored brown and white whiskers, and only a few solid white ones. As expected, Tuxedo, a nine year old black and white shorthair, had solid black and solid white whiskers. Max, a red tiger of fourteen years, had very strange whiskers. On his right side they were mostly white with one very short black one. On his left side he had two short solid black and one very long smoky black one, the rest were all solid white. My other red tiger, a longhair named Nuke, had almost all black whiskers. Not a red whisker in the bunch. On an average there are between twelve and fifteen whiskers on each side of their nose.

Whiskers, scientifically known as vibrissae, aren't quite as important as the other sensory organs but they do have an important role. Whiskers work in concert with the other senses. They are special receptors designed to detect any changes in the cat's surroundings; tiny movements, air currents, air pressure changes, temperatures and wind direction.[1] They can tell the cat what is nearby, how big it is, and what direction it's in. In the dark, when vision is more limited, whiskers help the cat to feel where she is.

Whiskers are a very specialized form of hair. They are actually an extension of skin rather than just a normal hair. They are thicker and stiffer at the base and taper to a thin wisp at the tip. A domestic cat's whiskers are twice as thick as her long guard hairs. Whiskers grow from a special skin follicle strengthened by a fibrous capsule and each whisker extends almost three times deeper into the skin than the normal hairs. The specialized hair follicles lie in a skin bed that is richly supplied with blood vessels and nerve endings. The follicles are connected to small muscles, the arrector pili muscles, which allow movement. Each whisker is connected to nerve endings that transmit signals to the cat's brain.

There are several areas, on the cat's face, of whiskers, each with its own purpose. From top to bottom they are, eye whiskers, cheek whiskers and mouth-chin whiskers. The whiskers above, and to the sides of, the eyes, eye whiskers, are thinner than the rest. They are known as superciliary and genal tufts. There are normally about three or four longer ones with five to six others about half as long. These act as feelers but would aid in eye protection from dust particles as well.

The cheek whiskers, also known as mystacial tuft, are the main vibrissae. They act as side feelers. The cat can use these to gauge width of passage. In other words, if her whiskers fit so will the rest of her body. I am reminded of my cat, Miss Kitty, when she was pregnant, her whiskers stood out further and straighter than when she wasn't pregnant. Younger kittens have more whiskers, both cheek and eye, than adults. Therefore their feeler needs must be greater. There are four rows of cheek whiskers on each side of the nose. The second rows are the longest, the first and third rows are the same length, and the fourth rows (bottom) are the shortest. The bottom rows extend further in toward the mouth. The second and third rows have more whiskers in them. Cats appear to be able to move two rows of whiskers independently of each other, the top two rows separately from the bottom two rows. This leads me to believe that there are two sets of additional muscles on each side.

Mouth-Chin whiskers, also known as mandibular tufts, are shorter and not as noticeable as the other areas. They cover around the mouth and the chin. Since the cat can't see directly under her nose, due to relationship of eye placement, the mouth-chin whiskers would help feel the nearness of things, i.e. important items of food, prey or drink.

Whisker positions are also important. The younger cat will hold, or rotate her whiskers forward most of the time because she is inquisitive, and feeling everything. An unhappy, or mad, cat will hold her whiskers back and flattened against her face. A happy cat, or a cat at rest will hold her whiskers out to the side. Sometimes the older cats will brush whisker tips with the younger ones, as in friendship.

The whiskers of my older cats tend to be more brittle and break periodically. Whiskers are also shed from time to time and do grow back. Older cats grow them back slower than younger cats. All thirty seven species of Felidae, the Cat Family, have whiskers but none to compare with those of our closer companion, the domestic cat.

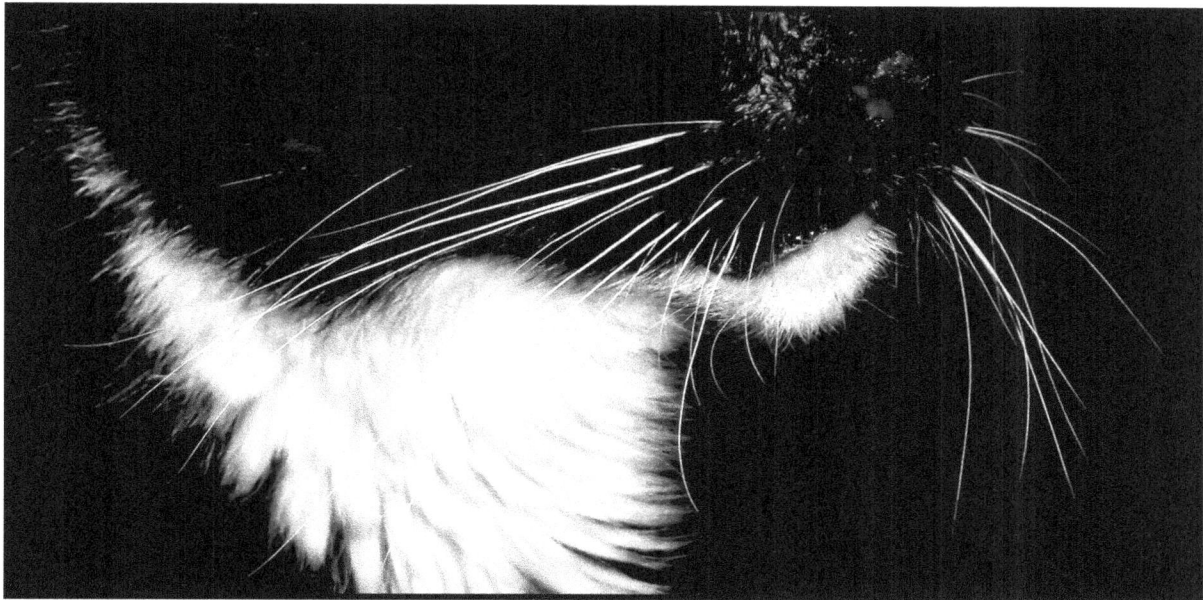

Photo by J. Lindley

These beautiful whiskers belong to Blackie Yang, age 10+ of Animal Helpline.

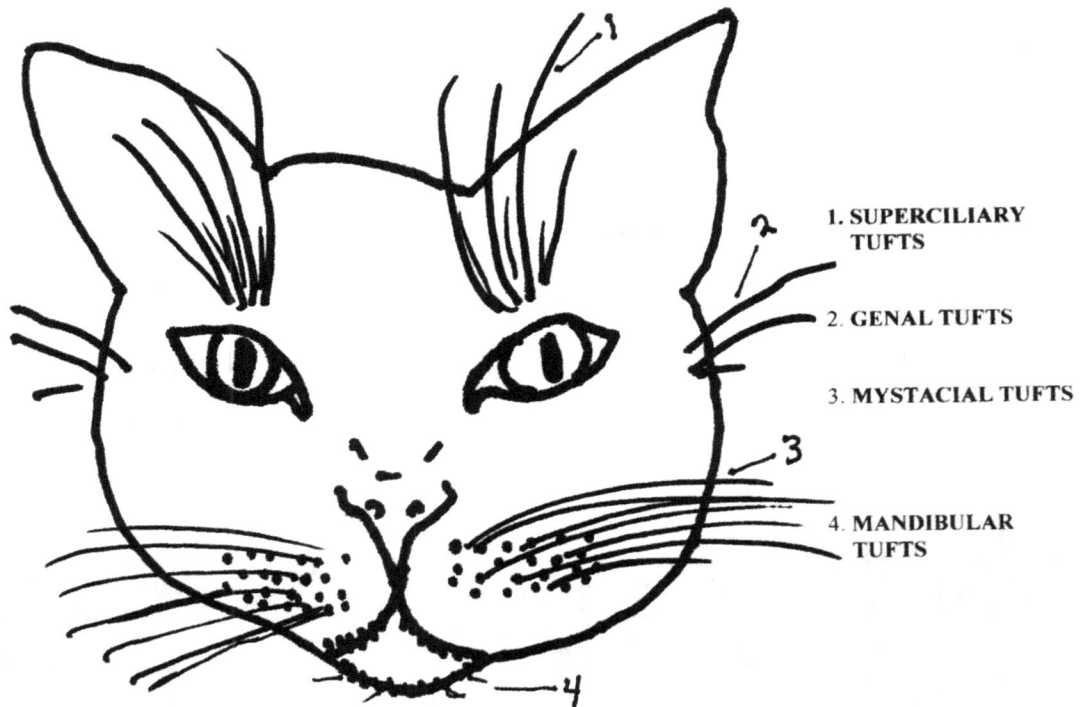

1. SUPERCILIARY TUFTS

2. GENAL TUFTS

3. MYSTACIAL TUFTS

4. MANDIBULAR TUFTS

THE CATS WHISKERS

NOTES

[1] *Wendy Christensen, "The Wondrous Whiskers", Cat Fancy Magazine (Dec. 1994): 32. Plus lots of personal observations - J. Lindley.*

5. MOUTH THE ORAL CAVITY, TEETH, GUMS AND TONGUE

"Through the lips and over the gums, watch out stomach, here it comes." The cat uses her mouth, the oral cavity, to capture prey, ingest food and to keep herself clean. The roof of the mouth is composed of the hard palate, a hard bony structure, and the soft palate, toward the back. At the very back of the mouth hangs the epiglottis. This fleshy extension prevents food from entering the windpipe during swallowing. The oral cavity houses the teeth, supported by the gums, and the largest organ of taste, the tongue.

Food, entering the mouth, is grasped, torn and chewed (masticated) by the teeth. Saliva, secreted by the salivary glands (located under the tongue, at the back and beneath the lower jaw and within the oral mucousa membrane, the cheek lining), moistens the food for easier swallowing. Enzymes in the saliva begin the food breakdown. The tongue moves the food around, during chewing, to form a food bolus. Then, the tongue moves backward pushing the food into the throat for swallowing.

The adult cat has a total of thirty teeth: incisors, six upper and six lower; canines, two upper and two lower; premolars, six upper and four lower; and molars, two upper and two lower. The incisors are used for cutting food. The canines are the grabbing, tearing and holding teeth. The premolars and molars are gripping and grinding teeth. The teeth are held in place by the gums and jawbones.

Gums should be normally pink. Some cats may have black spots on them which is normal pigmentation. This black spotting, common in orange cats, is known as lentigo. Lentigo may be noticed on the lips, eyelids and nose as well as on the gums and it may increase in number with age.[1] It is common for adult cats to have a red line where the gums meet the teeth. This red line is characteristic of a sometimes mild gum disease known as gingivitis. Since older cats can tolerate mild gingivitis pretty well you may not ever notice they have it unless you look in their mouth. Gingivitis is caused by a buildup of plaque and tartar on the teeth, normally the premolars and molars, but sometimes on the canines. Bacteria in food particles, lodges in and around these teeth and combines with saliva to form plaque. Plaque hardens and forms tartar.[2] Unlike humans, where the tooth decays normally above the gum line, cats most often develop tooth decay just below the gum margins, causing gingivitis as well as cavities.[3] Signs of severe gingivitis are drooling, bad breath and pain or difficulty eating. She may jump back from her food as if she were stung by it.

With age, the gums can recede, causing the teeth to become loose or fall out. In some cases, particularly in cats 11 years and older, the canine teeth will drop down giving the appearance of vampire fangs. Teeth may also become brittle and break. Fortunately, older cats can manage extremely well with only a few teeth. I have a seventeen year old who has only one premolar on each side and she still prefers to crunch dry cat food. Dry cat food, because of the abrasive action, will actually aid in keeping the teeth clean. If your cat has most of her teeth but a problem with tartar buildup you may wish to have your veterinarian clean her teeth. Be sure to consult with your veterinarian how cleaning may be best done safely.

When comparing cats of various ages, I've noticed grain lines form in the canine teeth. A grain line is a line running the length, or grain, of the tooth. An eight year old may have one grain line; a fourteen year old will have two deep grain lines, sometimes a third coming in. Cats well into their twenties may have yellow, almost orange, and rounded teeth.[4] No matter what color or shape the teeth are in, their primary function is chewing the food and, with the aid of the tongue, getting the food prepared for swallowing. Sometimes cats do appear to swallow without chewing, but they do chew.

The tongue, located on the floor of the oral cavity, is a very unique structure. The tongue has four primary functions; it aids in forming the food bolus and passes it towards the throat, it tastes the food with taste buds, it grooms and cleans the cat and it laps up liquids. The tongue is attached to the floor of the mouth by a fold of muscle tissue called the frenum linguae, which allows movement. On its surface are buds known as papillae. Unlike human's taste buds, located all over the tongue's surface, cat's taste buds are located only on the front and sides. These taste buds are called fungiform papillae and are mushroom-shaped. On the back of the tongue are cup-shaped taste buds called vallate papillae. The buds in the middle are not taste buds; they are used extensively for grooming. They are called filiform papillae and are sort of V-shaped to act like a comb while grooming.[5] The tongue, itself, is a muscular organ that can be shaped into a trough to lap or scoop up liquids favored by the cat.

Diseases, or health problems, of the oral cavity can begin on the lip. Sometimes seen on older cats, on the upper lip, usually opposite the canine tooth, is a bald or irritated spot, called a rodent ulcer. This is called such because it was once thought these ulcers were caused by the bite of a rodent. Although rodent ulcers do most commonly occur on the lip they can also appear on the roof of the mouth, back of the throat and on the tongue. In the mouth they are usually raised with a rough surface, red or yellow in color and circular shaped.[6] They can be treated.

One form of cancer that can affect the oral cavity is seen as a malignant tumor and is called squamous cell carcinoma. It may affect the gums, oral mucous membranes (cheek linings) and the underside of the tongue. It may resemble ulcers rather than lumps.[7] It can be treated with radiation or be surgically removed. It is progressive so see your veterinarian early. Of all the infections of the oral cavity the worst is peridontal disease. It ranks among the most common diseases of pets and is most severe in cats.[8] This disease ranges in severity from gingivitis (red gums) to loss of supporting bone structure.[9] Because of the pain involved your cat will refuse to eat or drink. Weight loss and dehydration can become a problem, which is disastrous for an older cat.

Signs of all oral problems are pretty much the same; drooling, bad breath, sensitivity, pain when eating and even out and out refusal to eat or drink. If you notice any of these signs see your veterinarian.

Normal problems of the aging cat are dry mouth, due to lack of saliva production, receding gums and slower or difficult swallowing, due to aging muscle tone (in more advanced years).

Your health care should include periodic home examination of the teeth and gums, at which time you can also check the tongue. Dry food, even if given only part time, is good because of its abrasive action, while chewed it helps reduce the tartar buildup.

Increased longevity in recent years may be, in part, due to better care of teeth and gums and from awareness of possible problems by both pet owners and veterinarians alike.

There is an old saying "the healthier your cat's mouth is, the greater the well-being of your cat."

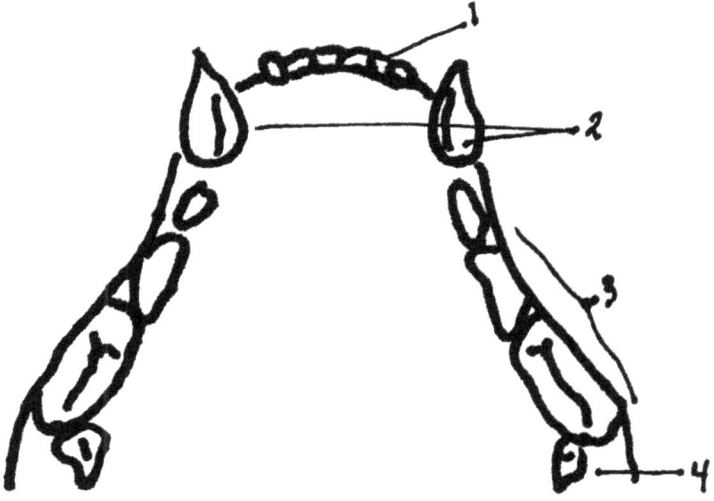

1. INCISORS

2. CANINES

3. PREMOLARS

4. MOLAR

R   UPPER   L

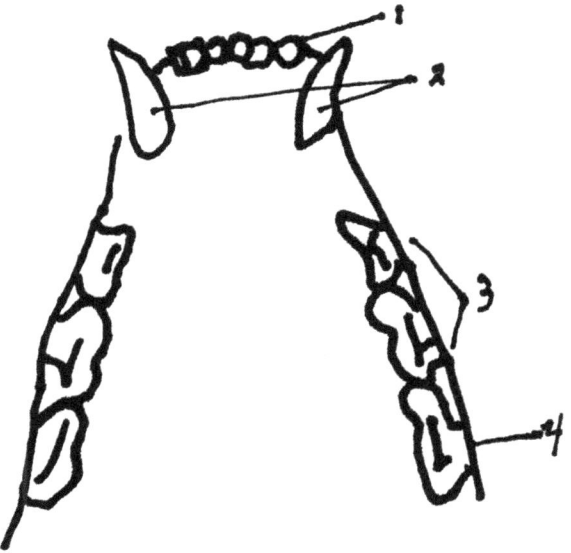

1. INCISORS

2. CANINES

3. PREMOLARS

4. MOLAR

L   LOWER   R

THE CAT'S TEETH

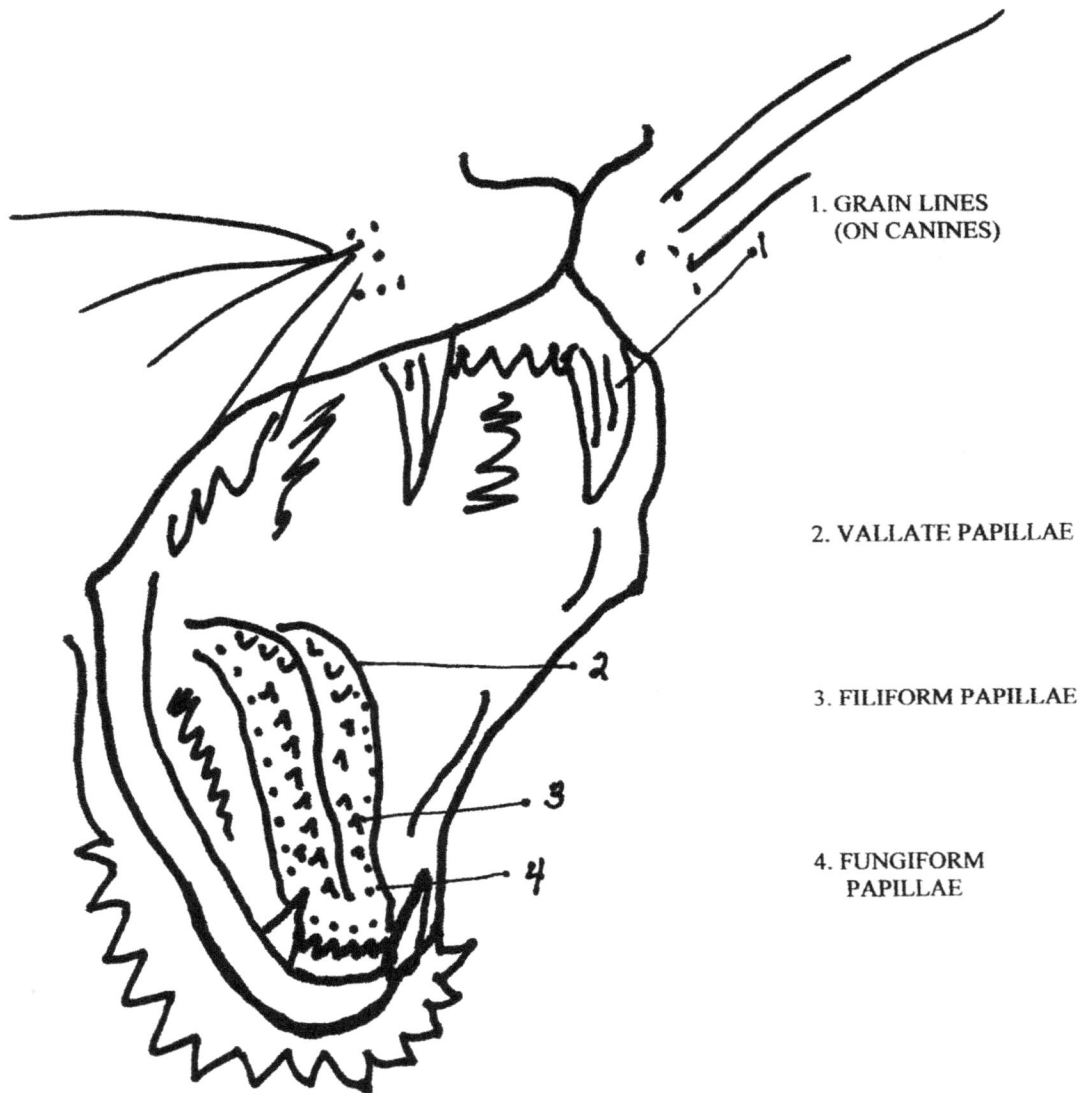

1. GRAIN LINES (ON CANINES)

2. VALLATE PAPILLAE

3. FILIFORM PAPILLAE

4. FUNGIFORM PAPILLAE

THE ORAL CAVITY

NOTES

[1] *George H. Muller, Robert W. Kirk and Danny W. Scott, Small Animal Dermatology, 4th Ed (Philadelphia: W. B. Saunders Co. 1989): 707.*

[2] *Margie Kacoha and James P. Cook Jr., "Dental Care For Cats", Cat Fancy Magazine (March 1987): 50.*

[3] *Jeffrey E. Barlough, Linda Susan Jorgensen and Ronald C. Riis, Sensory Organs and Disorders, The Cornell Book of Cats (N.Y.: Villard Books, div of Random House 1992): 163.*

[4] *Grain lines and old teeth - personal observation -J. Lindley.*

[5] *Thomas G. Morrisey, "Catanatomy", Cornell's Feline Health Center's Perspective On Cats (Summer 1990): 4.*

[6] *Tim Haecroft, The Howell Book of Cat Care (N.Y.: Howell, 1991): 164.*

[7] *Jeffrey E. Barlough, Linda Susan Jorgensen and Ronald C. Riis, Sensory Organs and Disorders, The Cornell Book of Cats (N.Y.: Villard Books, div of Random House, 1992): 163.*

[8] *Animal Health Newsletter, Cornell University College of Veterinary Medicine (March 1987): 2*

[9] *Catnip, Newsletter of Tufts University School of Veterinary Medicine (August 1994): 5.*

6. SKIN AND COAT

They say 'Beauty is only skin deep'. This is not so with the cat. In good health her coat is truly a thing of beauty. In older years, and especially in poor health, her skin and coat is a mirror of what's wrong inside, as well as what may be affecting her from the outside.

The skin and its associated structure, the hair are part of the integumentary system. Unlike the other senses, previously discussed, the skin serves in many different ways. It protects the cat from water loss and absorption, from physical abrasion and, with the hair, from harmful effects of the sun. It is also a defense against outward parasites, insects and allergens, such as pollen. The skin and coat give aid as camouflage. Receptors in the skin receive information of heat and cold. With this information the skin can help regulate the body's temperature.[1] Since cats don't sweat like humans do they are provided with another unique ability. As the temperature rises it triggers a saliva gland to water copiously. The cat spreads the saliva on her coat for water vaporization, and cooling results.[2] Lastly, the skin, through a very special process and with the help of the sun, makes vitamin D,[3] which is very important for strong bones.

The skin is composed of layers, the epidermis (top layer), the dermis (inner layer) and the subcutaneous (under layer). The epidermis is made up of several layers of cells with the thickness determined by position, i.e. paws or back being thicker for added protection. The inner layer of epidermal cells is constantly dividing, pushing the older cells toward the surface, so the surface is thicker. These surface cells contain keratin, a waterproofing protein, which prevents water loss and protects against invading organisms.

The dermis is composed of connective, nervous and muscle tissue. Many arteries, veins and capillaries are in the dermis. Within the dermis are the proteins collagen, which provides strength, and elastin, which provides stretch. The muscle tissue, the arrector pili muscle, is attached to the hair follicles, penetrating the dermis, allowing the hair to stand on end. This is particularly handy when the cat is afraid or angry; she uses these muscles to make her hair stand, and increasing her appearance in size almost two fold, to scare off the intruder. The connective tissue surrounds each hair follicle.

The last layer, the subcutaneous layer, connects the skin to the deeper structures. This is the layer that enables the movement of the skin separate from the lower tissues. This layer also has the fat, or adipose, tissues. This is the fat layer that keeps the cat warm.

Within the skin, in certain areas, are specialized types of glands, which secrete fluids through the skin. The cat has two types of sweat glands, eccrine and apocrine glands. The eccrine are the true sweat glands, located on the pads of the nose and paws. Although cats get warm all over, they sweat mostly through their paw pads, leaving a trail of damp paw prints. The apocrine glands are found mostly in areas where the hair is less dense, such as cheeks, chin, forehead and base of tail. They are a type of scent gland, rather than a sweat gland, as they secrete materials that are most likely used for recognition, establishing territory and sexual attraction.[4] In the female, mammary glands, located on the belly-side, secrete milk.

The hair, or coat, of your cat is very special. It comes in a variety of lengths, short to long and styles, straight to wavy and curly and whatever its length or style its function is the same. It serves as added protection, to the skin, from injury (by deflection), cold and harmful effects of the sun (by insulation). The overall condition of your cat's coat serves as an indicator of good health. A sick cat will not properly groom herself, leaving the coat looking clumpy.

The coat is made up of individual hairs, or hair shafts. The hairs grow from tiny holes in the skin called follicles. There may be as many as 130,000 hair follicles per square inch of the cat's body.[5] With each hair follicle is an oil gland, the sebaceous gland, that, when pressed by its connected arrector pili muscle, causes the oil to flow out and lubricate the hair for protection. This oil film also helps keep the skin soft as well as keeping the hair flexible and the coat lustrous. The overall coat is made up of two types of hair coats, the outer coat and the inner coat. The outer coat has the long guard hairs and medium sized hairs, called awn hairs. The inner coat is made up of shorter and finer hairs, down hairs. When the skin senses cold it uses the arrector pili muscles to contract and fluff the outer coat which traps a layer of warm air next to the inner coat and skin. This action insulates the cat.

Hair is situated, in the skin layer, within a follicle, a column of cells, with a swollen base, made partially of connective tissue. Hair, itself, is made up of two parts, the shaft (which projects above the skin surface) and the root, at the base of the follicle. The hair shaft is made up of three parts, cuticle, cortex and medulla. The cuticle is the outer scale-like covering. The cortex is the middle area containing melanin, the color pigment. The medulla, the inner area, contains cells with air spaces or protein, which will turn into keratin. The color is determined by the amount of melanin present in the cortex of the hair shaft, and in the cells of the skin.[6] The more dense the melanin the darker the color. Gray hair is loss of pigment and white hair is air in the hair shaft.[7] The amount of pigment produced reduces with age so gray hair may be present. Similarly the cells in the medulla die and leave air pockets causing white hair. Cats, unlike dogs, have only a very few, if any, gray or white hairs added with age. You may notice it around the muzzle of an older Siamese cat.

As people become wrinkled with old age so, in a way, do cats. Cats with very little hair, such as the Sphynx, will actually show folds of loose and wrinkled skin. Cats with denser hair will just show looser skin. The main reasons for this is loss of muscle tone in the elasticity of the skin tissue (lack of elastin in the dermis) and loss of fat from the subcutaneous layer. The reduction of body fat is what causes the older cats to seek warm spots. They will lie in the only sunny spot in a room, around the heater or crawl under your bedcovers and nestle next to your warm body. Besides loss of fat there will be a loss of oil. The sebaceous glands will slowly cease to function causing the hair coat to become dry and brittle and the skin to be dry and flaky. The flaky skin gives the appearance of dandruff. The drying skin also causes the hair to shed more, becoming thinner and adding to the cat's desire for warmth.

As the cat ages she has a more difficult time grooming herself so this shedding can present problems. If the shedding hair is ingested by the cat, as she grooms, the hair can cause severe problems, and if not thrown up, or passed on through, they can be fatal. There are over-the-counter medications for hairball relief but I've always preferred regular butter, or margarine. A little butter offered on your finger will usually be licked off with great enthusiasm.

As the skin and coat age there may be several health problems. Aging causes a drop in the cat's immune, disease fighting, system so injuries, cuts or wounds, are slower to heal and are easily infected. The skin becomes more sensitive to allergens in the air, such as pollen, particularly grass pollens. A patchy coat or red itchy blistered skin may be the cat's reaction to this. Medications are available to soothe the reaction, but it's best to remove the cat from whatever caused her reaction. Eczema and dermatitis are evidenced by rashy areas and dry scaly skin. Patchy, or sparse hair, can be caused by several things, allergic reaction, nutritional deficiencies, and loss of hormones. Some cats will lose hair on their under-sides, belly area, and upper part of the inside back legs. This is called alopecia and is most likely caused by a hormone imbalance due to degenerating glands.[8] Vitamin B5 (Pantothenic acid) can help the hair grow back. It can be given orally or rubbed on the area. If your cat is eating a diet geared for older adults there should be little problems with hormonal or vitamin deficiencies.

The skin is the second most common location for cancer, in older cats, after the lymph glands.[9] The tumors come in various shapes from ulcerated, undefined areas, to solitary lumps. There are several types of tumors that may affect older cats, some benign and some malignant. Basal cell, squamous cell carcinoma, and fibrosarcoma are the three most common forms, usually occurring in older cats. Fibroma (connective tissue growth) and Lipoma (fat cell tumor) are also found in older cats and are usually benign. Mast cell tumor may be found in older male cats. Sebaceous gland and sweat gland tumors, although uncommon in cats, may occasionally be seen in older cats.[10] All of these form a tumor lump, just under the skin. Veterinarian diagnosis and surgical removal are necessary as some of these cancers can be malignant and spread to other tissues.

There are two forms of surface growths that may occur in older cats, papillomas and keratoses. Papillomas, cauliflower-like growths, may appear on the surface skin anywhere but especially on the face, eyelids and legs. If they interfere with your cat then they should be removed. Keratoses are actually an over abundance of keratin. They can appear as a red area or a crusted horny patch, or horny growth. They are most common on the ears and nose and usually do not interfere with the cat.

On the whole, skin tumors and growths are fairly uncommon in cats. But, a general rule of thumb is: If you find a lump while grooming, it's always best to have it checked by a veterinarian.

Daily grooming will help your cat immensely. The shed hair will be removed, rather than ingested, and your cat will enjoy your loving attention, showing that you still care for her even if she is getting older.

So, beauty is not just skin deep. Beauty is also a true sign of a healthy happy cat.

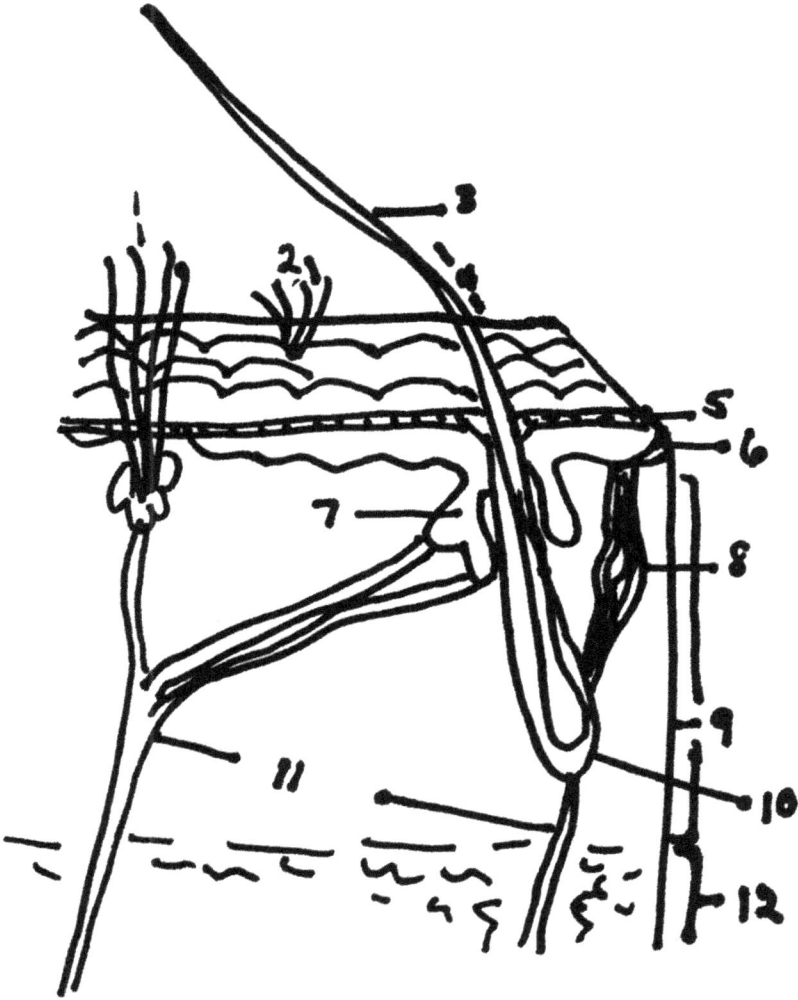

1. AWN HAIR
2. DOWN HAIR
3. GUARD HAIR
4. HAIR SHAFT
5. KERATIN CELLS
6. EPIDERMIS
7. SABACEOUS OIL
   GLAND
8. ARRECTOR PILI
   MUSCLE
9. DERMIS
10. HAIR FOLLICLE
11. CAPILLARIES
12. SUBCUTANEOUS
    LAYER

SKIN AND HAIR

NOTES

[1] *Animal Science, Anatomy and Physiology Part 2, (Scranton, PA: ICS Intangibles Holding Co, 1994): 36-37.*

[2] *Danny W. Scott, William H. Miller Jr., and Craig E. Griffin, Mueller & Kirk's Small Animal Dermatology, 5th Ed. (Philadelphia: W B Saunders Co, 1995): 43*

[3] *ibid,: 2.*

[4] *Danny W. Scott, Skin and Disorders. The Cornell Book of Cats. (N.Y.: Villard Books div of Random House, 1992): 145.*

[5] *"Cat's Haircoat: More Than Beauty", Purina News Service (Jan. 1995): 3.*

[6] *Animal Science, Anatomy and Physiology Part 2, (Scranton, PA: ICS Intangibles Holding Co., 1994): 39.*

[7] *ibid.*

[8] *Susan Kirchoff, "Long Lived Cats," Cat Fancy Magazine (July 1987): 54.*

[9] *Danny W. Scott, Skin and Disorders, The Cornell Book of Cats (N.Y.: Villard Books div of Random House, 1992): 159.*

[10] *ibid.*

7. OF CLAWS AND PAWS

"You show me your teeth and I'll show you my claw!"

Claws are an extension of the skin, the integumentary system. An average cat has eighteen claws. They are hard protective keratinized coverings used primarily for the cat's protection, either from animal (including human) intruders or external parasites, ie. fleas and ear mites. Little kittens use their claws to hang onto things. Adult cats use their claws to help stretch their toe muscles, as well as shoulder and leg muscles. Claws are also used to catch and grasp prey. However, the primary function the claws are most recognized for is the cat's personal defense.

Claws are made up of two sections the epidermis (or cuticle) and the dermis (or quick). The outer layer, the cuticle, grows continuously so it must be shed. The cat usually takes care of this by scratching, hopefully on a scratching post, or pad, or at least carpet (if inside). The inner layer, the dermis, or quick, contains nerves and blood supply. If a cat tears a claw, or if it's cut improperly, this area will bleed and be very sensitive to your cat. As the cat ages her claws become thicker, sometimes the rear claws more so than the front. They tend to catch on carpets. The older cats have more problems with this catching as their claws don't retract as readily as they did at a younger age, due in part to aging muscles. Cats can pull off the outside layer themselves but it takes a certain amount of strength, with the thicker claw, and sometimes the older cat just doesn't want to bother doing it.

If the claws are not kept properly they may become torn and infected. They can also continue to grow in toward the foot pad and cause severe pain. Trimming the claw is not hard. Clipping the points usually does it. Be careful not to clip into the quick. Older cats who don't want to be held to do this should be taken to a groomer or your veterinarian. Pay close attention to the condition of your cat's claws. If one claw is different it may indicate trauma, infection or even a tumor. If all four paws look strange see your veterinarian right away. This could be an indication of systemic diseases, feline leukemia, feline immunodeficiency virus, or diabetes, hyperthyroidism, Cushings Syndrome or possible nutritional deficiencies.[1]

I thought there might be a noticeable difference in color or condition in comparison of my younger cat's (age 4) claws and older cat's (age 16) claws. They both seemed to be as translucent and equally as sharp. Both cats are house cats and have equal access to scratching pads and carpets (for claw shedding) as well as door jams (for sharpening).

The claws are sheathed by the paw. The most unique feature of this velvety sheath is the fact that it affords the claw retractability. The claw is held in place by two small bones (the distal phalanx) which are folded. When the cat extends her claws she tightens a tendon which unfolds these bones, straightening them out, thus pushing the claw forward and downward, and at the same time, spreading the toes. This spreading action not only increases the size of the paw but uncovers its razor-like knives, the claw.

Besides housing the claw the paw has many other functions. The paw is your cat's hand, foot, weapon, 'landing gear' and marking tool. The toes of the paw are called digits. The toe pads are called digital pads. The large pad is called the metacarpal pad. The smaller pad on the front leg is the carpal pad. The carpal pad is only used in landings; otherwise it hardly ever touches the ground. The digital and metacarpal pads not only act as cushions but have other special purposes. These pads contain a network of capillaries that help radiate excess body heat, in the form of sweat, to cool the cat's body. In addition, located in these pads are special scent glands. The cat rubs her paws on things to leave her scent on them. The next time your cat rubs your cheek with her chin, cheek or paw, you might want to think about why she does it. Is she labeling you as her possession? Maybe it's you who is owned rather than vice-a-versa.

The older cat loses moisture from within the paw pads. In some cases they not only shrink in size but become callused and dry, or worse, cracked.[2] As the older cat still spends a lot of time on her feet, the paws bear the weight so pad condition is important. Older cats also use more paw and leg area than younger cats. They become more flat-footed. This flat-footed appearance is due to aging body joints which cause an overall body slope but is most noticeable in the feet. I've also noticed that the paws, of the older cat, particularly the rear ones, lose moisture in the skin of the toes. The skin tightens and pulls back exposing more of the claw, adding to the catching problem.

Included in your daily observance of your aging cat should be listening for clicking claws as she crosses your kitchen floor (an indication of claws too long) and watching for any signs of limping or foot tenderness. Your aging baby may need to rely on you for foot care.

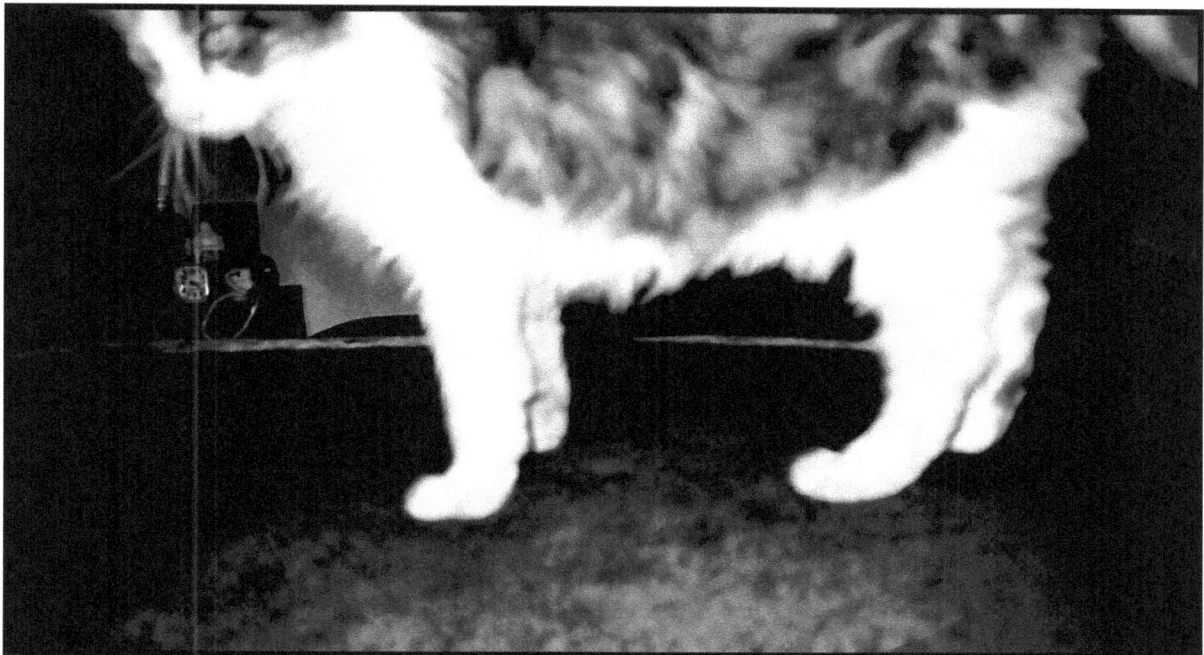

Photo by J. Lindley

My retiree, C.J. (yes named after a jeep) at 17 years is a fine example of 'older' feet. Notice how much foot area is utilized.

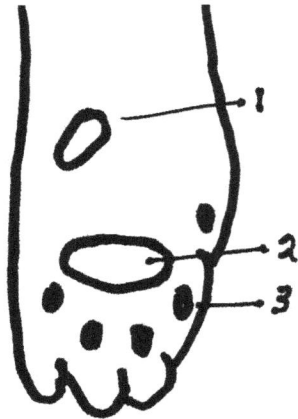

FRONT PAW (5 TOES)

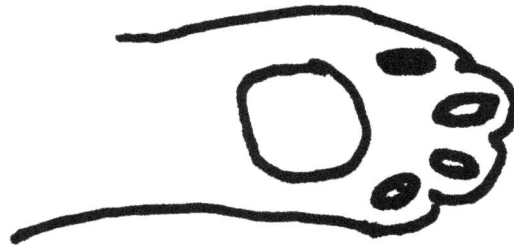

1. CARPAL PAD

2. METACARPAL PAD

3. DIGITAL PADS

BACK PAW (4 TOES)

1. PAW

2. EPIDERMIS (CUTICLE)

3. DERMIS (QUICK)

4. CLIPPING LINE
   About a 45 degree angle

PAWS And CLAWS

NOTES

[1] Kathy Salzberg, "Scratching Out the Truth on Paws and Claws," *Cat Fancy Magazine*, (Feb. 1995): 55.

[2] *Personal observation, J. Lindley.*

8. DEM BONES THE SKELETAL-MUSCULAR SYSTEM

"Dem bones, dem bones, dem jive bones." In the older cat they still jive just not quite as good as they used to.

The cat's skeletal system consists of bones, ligaments, tendons and cartilage. The ligaments join bone to bone, at a joint, the tendons join bone to muscle and the cartilage covers the ends of bones, at a joint, while it also forms pads, or discs, between the spinal vertebrae.

Bones are made up mostly of calcium. The long, major limb bones are composed of dense bone with compartment-like spongy bone at the ends and a hollow marrow-filled center. The bones are covered by a thin membrane, the periosteum, to which the ligaments and tendons attach. The overall skeletal system has approximately 244 bones[1] whose primary function is to give support and protection to the cat's body be serving as a framework.

The major part of the skeleton is the spinal vertebrae. They are short irregular shaped bones and there are between 44 and 58 of them, depending on the length of the cat's tail. They are 7 neck (cervical), 13 chest (thoracic), 7 back (lumbar), 3 pelvic (sacral) and 14 to 28 tail (caudal) bones.[2] The primary function of the vertebrae is to encase and protect the spinal cord, with secondary function of providing support to a large portion of the cat's body.

A very special part of the skeletal system, an extension of the vertebrae, with many of its own unique attributes is the cat's tail. The tail, or caudal bones, comprise about one third of the entire vertebrae.[3] Depending on breed of cat, they vary in length. The tail bones are connected more loosely together to enable a variety of movement. The tail acts as a rudder and a counterweight, especially when leaping or pouncing. A shift of the tail can change the center of gravity and the direction of the cat, just like the rudder on a boat.

Some older cats are sensitive to touch at their tail-body connection. This may be a result of past injury, possibly pulling too hard, causing strained muscles or even fractured tail bones. Normally cats like to be scratched at the tail connection. The normal expected response is a tail lift and slightly arched back, while standing high on their back toes.

Tail positions vary with the age of cat. Young cats, being inquisitive, stretch out and hold their tails all the way out and flat to the floor when investigating. Cats of mating age hold their tails in a more prominent stiffer manner as if to say they are very confident of themselves. An angry cat slowly lashes her tail before attacking. A frightened cat pulls her tail in between her hind legs. Older cats hold their tails in a more relaxed position but slightly lower than when they were younger. The thing I like best about the cat's tails is the way they twitch them while enjoying birds through a window. All sleeping cats, when in a curled position, bury their nose in their tail. The tail not only keeps their feet warm but, by covering the nose, reduces the oxygen intake and induces a deeper sleep.[4] Tails have their own set of specific problems. They run the gamut from bald or patchy spots to tail chewing. A drooping tail is usually a signal that the cat isn't feeling quite up to par.

As the cat ages many bone changes take place. The aging digestive system absorbs more calcium and phosphorus, both desperately needed by the bones, from the body system.[5] The bones become thinner and brittle allowing them to become easily broken, fractured, or dislocated. The fluid in the joints reduces causing the bone end cartilage to dry. The cartilage discs between the vertebrae lose their flexibility and dry out leaving the body open to a number of bone problems, the most common of which is arthritis.

Arthritis, specifically osteoarthritis, is a degenerative joint disease that can become an extremely chronic problem with older cats.[6] Not all old cats get this but those who do may become lame or severely sway-backed. This condition is caused by deterioration at the bone joints. When a limb is afflicted, the cartilage end surface of long bones becomes rough, pitted and worn away.[7] Movement of an afflicted joint eventually results with the bone wearing away as well. When the vertebrae are afflicted, bony proliferation (excess bone growth) can take place, throwing the vertebrae totally out of line. All the joints involved become inflamed and very painful. Added to this, the muscles in the involved area become overtaxed and weaken, causing painful movement, slowness and lameness.

Cats can be very stubborn and they can hide their pain extremely well. I had a cat, Moxy, who had a very mild case of osteoarthritis. She just seemed a little slow and stiff at first. Then a week before she 'left' me, at the age of nearly twenty years, she became extremely sway-backed and crouched in the hindquarters. Still every morning she came down the hall to get me to come to the kitchen and feed her. Thoughts of euthanasia crossed my mind but, she was so full of life and seemed so happy, I just couldn't steal her last days. It is said that animals can cut off pain to a certain area so, that's what she must have done.

Unfortunately, there is no cure for osteoarthritis as it is a degenerative condition. There are medicines available, through your veterinarian, to reduce pain. NEVER give your cat aspirin or Tylenol®, they can build up in the cat's system and be fatal. Sometimes rubs containing menthol or oil of camphor can be soothing. DO NOT use any products containing phenol. Phenol is very poisonous to cats. It's always best to check with your veterinarian before giving any pain relief medicine.

Tumors (neoplasts) of the skeletal system are not common in cats. There are no particular tumors related to only older cats. They do occasionally occur[8] and, depending on the type, will be sensitive in the area involved. If you notice anything unusual it's best to see your veterinarian as soon as possible.

The skeletal system is provided movement by the muscular system, hence the name skeletal-muscular system. The muscles that move the skeleton are called skeletal muscles. They are striped, or striated, fibrous tissue formed in bands to allow contraction. They are usually found in pairs so that they contract alternately causing movement. The cat's body has approximately 250 paired muscles.[9] The muscles are attached to the bones by tendons. Muscles give the cat's body locomotion. Just try to tell an older cat she has to slow down and see how 'loco' she becomes. Cats only seem to slow down when they are reminded to, usually by stiffness or lameness.

Normal degenerative problems with muscles occur due to slowing circulation, poor oxygen supply, causing them to overwork, possibly stretch and become sore. In extreme cases they may draw up, cramp, adding to lameness. As the muscles become weaker so do the tendons. Tumors of the muscular system are rare in cats.[10]

Falls can be particularly dangerous for an older cat. Leaping can cause pulled muscles and strained tendons but, even worse, the improper landings can cause broken, dislocated bones, and slipped discs. If your cat injures her back you may wish to consult a chiropractor. Chiropractics, applied to animals, is becoming popular, although sometimes controversial, and in many cases the chiropractor will work directly with your veterinarian. Chiropractics are based on the premise that the joints, specifically the spinal joints, cause the least problems when they are in proper position.[11] If the vertebra is in proper alignment, the nerves and the blood supply to the body will be proper - at least operate as properly as possible. There is no need for anesthesia. Through applied heat, warm hands, and massage the dislocated bones can be realigned comfortably. This is great for the older cat.

To help your older cats cope with aging bones and muscles watch for signs of stiffness, lameness or refusal to move. Sometimes a brisk brushing and gentle whole-body massage can do wonders. Remember the "Midas Touch"? Well, your touch is pure gold to your cat. Regular activity is often a key to keep ahead of stiffening joints and muscles. Try string toys. They will give your cat an opportunity to properly exercise those tiring muscles and have fun doing it. You'll be surprised how much fun your cat can have even with an old shoelace.

Cats afflicted with osteoarthritis should be kept warm, dry and have a soft place to rest their sore bones. They seem to favor a more upright sleeping position, resting their head on their front paws, rather than the more normal curled sleeping position. A severely arthritic cat will rest, more often, on her side, to ease the weight on her sore back. The foam filled mats, or large padded pet beds work well for older cats. My older cats like my bed or the large, soft dog bed, where three or more can rest together. Guess they know it's not too awful to get old, especially when you have company to share it with. Sometimes growing older can be a real pain, for all of us, unfortunately it's something we all must deal with but at least we can be there for each other.

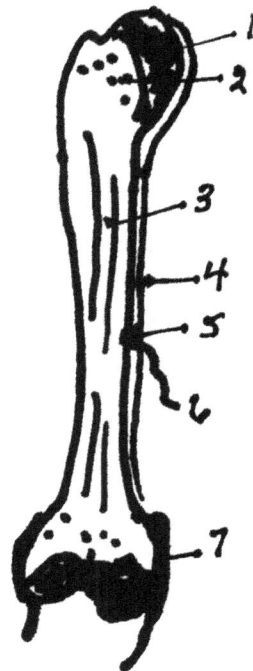

NORMAL BONE

1. CARTILAGE

2. SPONGY BONE

3. DENSE BONE

4. PERIOSTEUM

5. OPENING FOR BLOOD SUPPLY

6. BLOOD SUPPLY

7. LIGAMENT

OLDER BONES & JOINTS

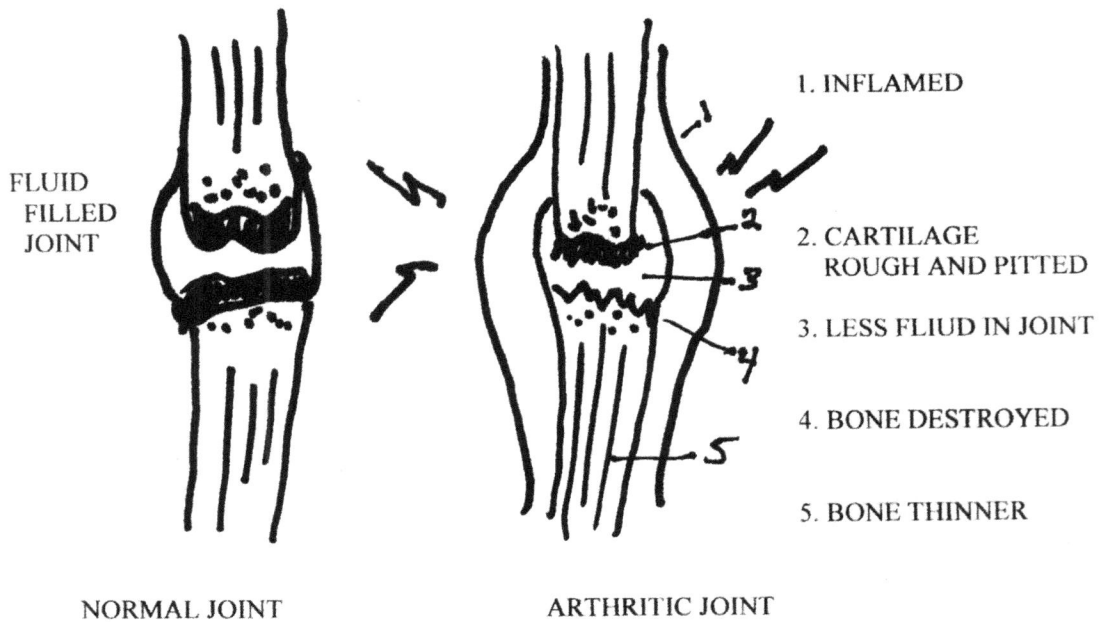

FLUID FILLED JOINT

1. INFLAMED

2. CARTILAGE ROUGH AND PITTED

3. LESS FLIUD IN JOINT

4. BONE DESTROYED

5. BONE THINNER

NORMAL JOINT

ARTHRITIC JOINT

CHANGES IN THE BACK

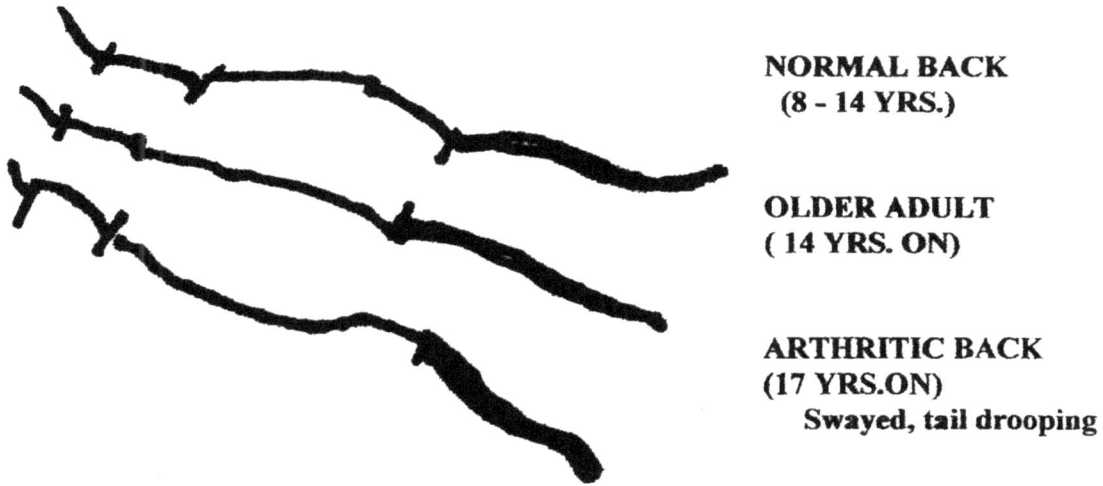

NORMAL BACK
(8 - 14 YRS.)

OLDER ADULT
(14 YRS. ON)

ARTHRITIC BACK
(17 YRS.ON)
   Swayed, tail drooping

STAGES OF OSTEOARTHRITIS OF THE BACK

1. Cats walk more slowly and carefully, being careful not to jar themselves.

2. The back, particularly before the tail, begins to sway

3. Back very swayed. Movement will be hunched down in the hindquarters, with more weight on the hind lower legs. Refusal to leave sleeping area. Only moving if necessary to eat, drink or use the litter box. Will strongly object to being lifted.

NOTES

[1] *Wendy Christensen, "The Cat's Revealing Tail," Cat Fancy Magazine (Mar. 1995): 10.*

[2] *"Landing On All Fours" (Skeleton), Catnip, Newsletter of Tufts University School of Veterinary Medicine (Oct. 1993): 1.*

[3] *Same as 1 cited above.*

[4] *Same as 1 cited above - page 11.*

[5] *June Kirvan Tuttle, Jeffrey E. Barlough, Mordecai Siegal and Leo A. Wuori, Aging Cats and Disorders, The Cornell Book of Cats. (N.Y.: Villard Books div of Random House, 1992): 312.*

[6] *Jeffrey E. Barlough, Musculoskeletal System and Disorders, The Cornell Book of Cats (N.Y.: Villard Books div of Random House, 1992): 202.*

[7] *ibid.*

[8] *ibid: 203.*

[9] *Animal Science, Anatomy and Physiology Part 1 (Scranton, PA: ICS Intangibles Holding Co., 1994): 21. and Fernand Mery, The Life, History and Magic of the Cat, (N.Y.: Madison Square Press 1968): 118*

[10] *Same as 8. cited previously.*

[11] *Alan C. Breen, Chiropractics, A Visual Encyclopedia of Unconventional Medicine (N.Y.: Crown Pubs 1979): 73.*

9. PURR AND THE INTERRUPTED PURR

It's hard to say really if a purr is an outward change or an inward change. Although, the purr is definitely produced on the inside it is an external auditory sound. Since the purr normally accompanies a cat's external position I have chosen this chapter to discuss - the purr and the interrupted purr.

The Webster's New World Dictionary describes purr as "purr (pur) n. [echoic] a low, vibratory sound made by a cat at ease - vt. to make, or express by, such a sound."[1] Good description but not altogether accurate. Those of us 'cat people' know that a cat not only purrs when she is comfortable but will also purr when she is frightened.

Purr is the sound the kitten first hears, or feels, from her mother while she nurses. In response, the kitten purrs back and she feels secure and safe. Purr is the sound made by the adult cat as she lies, secure and safe, in your lap. Purr is the sound your cat makes as she sits across from you, a sound of simple affection. I do not fully understand why my cats purr while sitting on the veterinarian's table. Perhaps they're telling me that even if they're not feeling well they're glad that I'm with them. Simply put, purr cat's way of saying "I LOVE YOU".

There are several theories to explain how a cat purrs. What I found strange was that all the authoritative books on the subject of Purr either discuss all the theories or skirt the issue entirely. The earliest theory, Fernand Mery (1966), says that it is "probably" produced by the vibrations of one of the two vocal cords of the cat's throat.[2]

The next theory, the vena cava theory, suggests that purring is the result of turbulence in the bloodstream of the vena cava (the main vein returning blood from the body to the heart). According to this theory, the cat arches her back, which causes the blood to rush against the walls, of the narrowest part of the vena cava, where it passes through the cat's liver and diaphragm, causing vibrations in the chest that resonate, via windpipe, in the sinus cavities of the cat's head.[3] This is a good theory, but cats must arch their back to cause this and they do not always do so immediately preceding the purr. One of my cats, Silver Streak (affectionately known as Sliver), purrs as soon as she sees me no matter what position she's in.

The last theory (reported by Drs. Lea Stogdale, BVSc, and John B. Delack, DVM, PhD., of Canada in Cornell's Newsletter of July 1986) states that purring is controlled by an oscillatory mechanism in the cat's central nervous system, which causes a regular rapid, alternating activation of muscles of the larynx and the diaphragm. The purring is produced by changes in the glottis, the cat's vocal cords. They recorded, with electromyograms, three distinct phases in every purr. The electromyograms measured activity associated with muscle contraction and recorded bits of purr associated with the cat's glottal opening, as it narrrows then opens rapidly. This causes change of pressure around the vocal cords and, in turn, they resonate causing the purr.[4] Cornell's Book of Cats (pg 53.) puts it more simply as purring being associated with rapid contractions of the muscles of the larynx and the diaphragm.[5]

Since my children are always curious about such things, especially those things related to their favorite cats, I consulted a child's book, More Big Book of Questions and Answers (1991). When asked, How Do Cats Purr? They responded with, the throat muscles relax and their vocal cords loosen. Breathing causes the cords to vibrate, making the purring sound. They go on to say that scientists report that frightened and angry cats also purr. The best statement they make is "Only a cat really knows how it purrs."[6] I tell my children the tale my grandfather told me, as a child, about a cat who was best friends with a mouse. They were best buddies until one day they had a great argument, most likely over food, and the cat ate the mouse. In revenge, the mouse rattles his bones every time the cat lies down to rest. Because of the seriousness of the betrayal of friendship the cat and all her descendants are cursed with the rattling bones.

Perhaps, they are all right. The purr may begin in the throat area and is enhanced by the cat arching her back as you stroke her. However, no matter what causes it, the purr is a valuable key to your cat's health. Normally a purr is an even rolling sound. A purr with interruptions of swallowing, coughing, sniffling, sneezing, wheezing or unusual popping sounds may be an indication of respiratory problems. The least of these will be allergies, but more serious may be bronchial diseases such as asthma, acute or chronic bronchitis and possible emphysema.

Asthma is a reversible obstruction of the airway, causing spasmodic contractions of the bronchi (tubes to the lungs).[7] It is caused by a response (either immunologic and/or neurologic) to a certain stimuli. An asthma attack may be brought on by litter dust, aerosol sprays, disinfectants and cigarette smoke. If your cat has an asthmatic reaction to something, see your veterinarian right away. Severe asthma attacks can cause a closing of the windpipe and it must be surgically opened. Asthma can occur at any age but mostly to young adults.[8] In older cats, the increasing number of seromucous bronchial glands and thick bronchial walls may increase the chance of asthma attacks.[9]

Acute bronchitis is an inflammation of the lungs usually caused by a bacterial infection and will normally respond to antibiotics. It can also occur in cats of any age.[10] If an older cat has had it before it may eventually become a chronic problem.

Chronic bronchitis is seen in middle to old age cats. Siamese cats may also be predisposed to this disease.[11] It is an inflammation of the lungs that is persistent. That means, even with treatments, the cat will still continue to get it. Signs of this are coughing, shortness of breath and wheezing. The damage of prolonged chronic bronchitis may be irreparable and the cat may wind up with emphysema.

Emphysema is a condition when air cannot be expelled from the lungs during normal breathing due to lost elasticity of the lung tissue, causing wheezing sounds. Although emphysema can occur in cats of any age it often follows chronic bronchitis.[12] My cat, Max, snores and wheezes in his sleep and during the day, he sniffles a lot. He is a possible candidate for emphysema, although at the moment he's being treated for multiple allergies.

When your cat is sleeping, listen for unusual sounds of snoring or wheezing. Older cats learn to hide their discomfort and pain well. Cats may actually purr to soothe themselves. Sometimes it isn't wise to just let sleeping cats lie. When your cat is awake you may notice interruptions in her purr. In this case your cat is not only saying, "I LOVE YOU", but "I may need your help", as well.

NOTES

[1] *Webster's New World Dictionary, (N.Y.: Warner Books, 1990): 478. Warner Books Paperback Ed.*

[2] *Fernand Mery, The Life, History and Magic of the Cat, N.Y.: Madison Square Press, 1968): 129.*

[3] *Barbera Diamond, "How Cats Purr", Cat Fancy Magazine, (June 1988): 56.*

[4] *"In Search of the purr-fect Explanation", Cornell 's Animal Health Newsletter (July 1986): 2.*

[5] *Katherine A. Houpt, Feline Behavior, The Cornell Book of Cats (N.Y.: Villard Books div of Random House, 1992): 53.*

[6] *Question: How Do Cats Purr?, More Big Book of Questions and Answers. (Lincolnwood, IL: Publications International Ltd, 1991): 58.*

[7] *June E. Tuttle, "Feline Bronchial Diseases", Cornell 's Perspectives on Cats (Summer 1990): 1*

[8] *ibid.*

[9] *Fred V. Scott, Respiratory System and Disorders, The Cornell Book of Cats (N.Y.: Villard Books div. of Random House, 1992): 224.*

[10] *June E. Tuttle, "Feline Bronchial Diseases", Cornell's Perspectives on Cats (Summer 1990): 1.*

[11] *ibid: 2.*

[12] *ibid.*

END CHART

Item	Normal	Aging	Illness
1. EYES	bright, clear	mild clear, watery discharge	messy, cloudy, mucus discharge
2. EARS	alert, clean	ender ear flaps doesn't respond to calling	shaking head, tilting ear or head, tilting unusual discharge
3. NOSE	clear, clean	mild, clear discharge possible sneezing	severe, mucus discharge, runny or clogged
4. WHISKERS	many positions	usually 2 positions relaxed, or flat if agitated	held back flat too often
5. MOUTH	white, sharp teeth, pink gums	mild gum line red teeth, grain lines sometimes broken or dulling very old: mild salivation, yellowing rounded teeth, tongue tip hanging out	red gums, or mouth tissues, swollen areas around teeth, tarter or plaque build-up, excessive drooling
6. SKIN & COAT	lustrous, regular shedding	dulling color, may feel dry, awn and down hairs feel softer, thinning coat, possible flaking skin, seeks warmth	extremely dull dry, brittle feel to coat, excessive shedding, balding areas, unusual scratching or grooming

Item	Normal	Aging	Illness
7. CLAWS & PAWS	regular scratching use of cat post and carpets, shedding thin claw covers	thickening claws, shed covers look thicker (all), catching in things, clicking on hard floors	dry, cracked bleeding pads, torn or bleeding claws, abnormal growth of claw
8. BONES & MUSCLES	body in normal high back position, active cat, tall, high and in many positions	regular to slowing activity, careful walking, lies in sun a lot, slightly sloping back, flat or flatter footed, tail in lower position	refusal to move, sway-backed, crouching or hunching position, tail drooping too often
9. PURR	loud, rolling	interrupted occasional purrs, more softer purr	severely interrupted, swallows while purrs

CHAPTER III INWARD CHANGES

In the study of Life Sciences there are two Kingdoms, Plant and Animal. The primary difference is what they utilize to live. Animals (including humans) breathe in oxygen and exhale carbon dioxide, while plants do the reverse. Each relies on the other.

Similarly, the internal systems of the cat rely on each other to operate properly. Oxygen is breathed in by the respiratory system, picked up by the circulatory system and carried throughout the rest of the body systems. Carbon dioxide, a waste of the cells, is circulated back to the respiratory system and released, or exhaled, into the air (to be utilized by plants). Food also taken in, by the cat, through the mouth, part of the digestive system, and necessary nutrients, is delivered to the other systems, the remaining unutilized waste products are eliminated by the urinary system and lower digestive system (the bowels). The last four systems influence, to some extent, all the others. The nervous system, with its primary organ the brain, has direct control over the cat's body organs. The endocrine system, glands and their secreted hormones, modify the other systems. The immune system is the health-keeper of all the body systems. Lastly, the reproductive system, if not already totally removed from the adult cat, can influence the health and life span of the cat.

The internal body organs of the cat age pretty much the same as the external organs. Moisture is lost causing the organ to wear out and malfunction, which, in turn, causes the related system to imbalance. Rather than discuss the organs separately, the systems are discussed. It is also important to notice that as each system slows down so does the natural immune system, leaving the older cat open to specific diseases of each system. Natural aging changes are referred to as a condition while any unnatural imbalance is considered a disease.

1. THE RESPIRATORY SYSTEM

It can be truthfully said that without breath there would be no life. Cats, like all other animals, require the intake of oxygen to live and this is provided by the Respiratory System.

The Respiratory System consists of: the nose (occasionally the mouth, if the nose is clogged); sinuses; throat (pharynx); voice box (larynx); windpipe (trachea); bronchi and lungs. Air, containing the precious oxygen, is breathed in (inhaled) through the nose, moistened and warmed by the sinuses, and turbinates, where it passes through the pharynx, and larynx into the trachea. The trachea divides into two passageways (bronchi) leading to the lungs. In the lung the bronchi branch into smaller passageways (bronchioles) which eventually end at an air sac (the alveolus or plural form, alveoli). Surrounding each air sac are capillaries, the smallest tubes containing blood. The inhaled oxygen passes through the cell membranes, of the alveoli, into the capillaries where it bonds to the red blood cells (hemoglobin) for transportation throughout the cat's body. At the time the oxygen is passed through the membrane, the body waste, carbon dioxide, is exchanged to be exhaled, or breathed out, and the entire passageway is repeated in reverse.

There are several things that can affect this oxygen passage, which can be due to natural breakdown of the aging cat and by diseases to the cat. All these slow down the air flow and result in health problems. At the top, nose level, is sinus breakdown. Already discussed with Outward Changes, Chapter II 3. Nose, sinus breakdown results in nasal discharge, clear or cloudy, that can clog up the nose and all but stop air passage. At this point the cat will breathe through her mouth. The nose is the respiratory system's first line of defense against dust, pollen and other potentially harmful particles that might be inhaled.[1] Of all the irritating things to the nose I think the worst are inhalant allergies. An allergy is the cat's immune response to an invading organism, an allergen. In the spring, we humans get 'hay fever.' Cats get 'hay fever' as well but it's known as allergic rhinitis and is due mostly to plant pollens, house dust and molds.[2] Symptoms of an allergy are a watery nasal discharge and sneezing. I've noticed that the older cats, with delicate sinuses, are more sensitive, to these allergens, than younger cats. There are medications available through your veterinarian to ease the symptoms. If left uncontrolled nasal discharges can be internal, as well as external, and can cause problems with the major organs of the respiratory system, the lungs. Natural breakdown of the lungs is attributed to replacement of working cells, of the alveolar lining, by connective fibrous tissue. This change causes the lungs to lose their elasticity and breathing is more difficult.[3] Another change, in the lungs, due to age is evidenced by the cilia, small hairs lining the bronchi, which move mucus and remove dirt from the lungs. The cilia actually cease to work, leaving the lungs open to disease.[4]

Diseases of the respiratory system fall into two categories: Upper respiratory (involving nose, sinuses, pharynx and larynx) and lower respiratory (involving trachea, bronchi and lungs).[5] Bronchitis and tracheitis (infections of the bronchi and trachea) are common respiratory problems in older cats (see Chapter II 9. PURR). If bronchitis isn't treated it can turn into chronic bronchitis and pneumonia. The older cat may have pulmonary edema or excess fluid in the lungs, due to a number of diseases particular to older cats, such as asthma, pneumonia, lung tumors, kidney disease and heart failure. Pulmonary edema occurs when the lymphatic system, the lymph cells in the blood system, is unable to remove all the excess fluid from the lungs.[6] Labored, rapid breathing through the mouth are symptoms of fluid build up. You should see your veterinarian right away, if you notice these symptoms. It could be a matter of life or death for your cat. Common symptoms of respiratory disease are sneezing, coughing and nasal discharge. Most infectious, virus type, respiratory diseases are covered by early vaccinations, while your cat is a youngster, then regular yearly boosters. Fortunately older cats, if properly vaccinated, will have built up their immune systems enough to be able to avoid most viruses. Follow your veterinarian's recommendations for vaccination schedule.

Whatever the cause, natural breakdown or disease, failure of the respiratory system with resulting overall lack of oxygen can cause two major problems. The muscles, receiving reduced oxygen, are unable to work properly and the cat's brain, also receiving insufficient oxygen, doesn't work as well either. Reduced oxygen to the brain causes the older cat to become disoriented and confused.[7] This confusion is evidenced by the cat wandering and crying at night.[8] Sometimes we are unable to do anything to help our aging babies, even though we dearly wish to. The best we can do is pick them up, hold them close and ride out the storm of age.

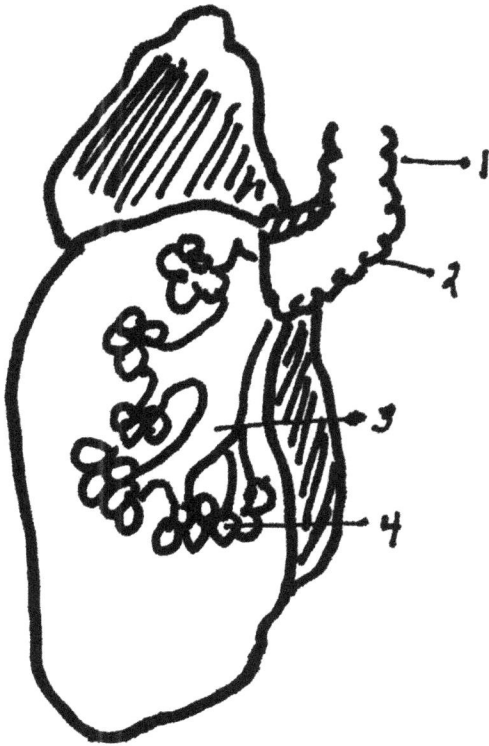

THE CAT'S LUNG

1. TRACHEA

2. BRONCHI

3. BRONCHIOLE

4. ALVEOLI

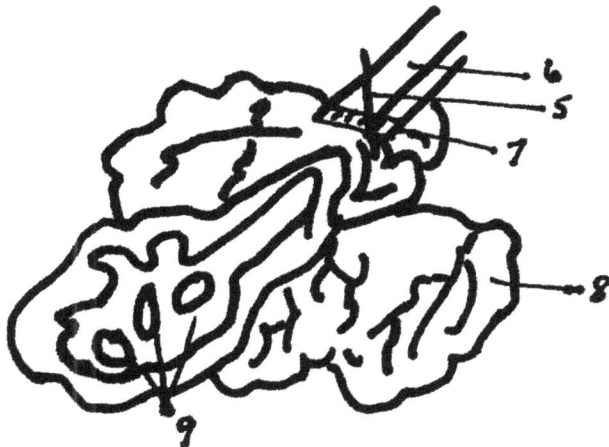

THE ALVEOLI

5. ARTERIOLE

6. BRONCHIOLE

7. MUSCLE TISSUE

8. ALVEOLUS

9. AIR SAC (INSIDE)

THE CAT'S RESPIRATORY SYSTEM

NOTES

[1] *Fred W. Scott, Respiratory System and Disorders, The Cornell Book of Cats (N.Y.: Villard Books div of Random House 1992): 219.*

[2] *Amy D. Shojai, "The Sensitive Nose", Cat Fancy Magazine (May 1994): 24.*

[3] *Robert Anderson, and BarbaraWrede, Caring for Older Cats and Dogs (Charlotte, VT: Williamson Pub. Co., 1990,: 46 &47.*

[4] *ibid.*

[5] *Fred W. Scott, Respiratory System and Disorders, The Cornell Book of Cats (N.Y.: Villard Books div of Random House 1992): 218.*

[6] *ibid: 224.*

[7] *Michael S. Bodri, Animal Science, Animal Care: Prenatal Through Old Age (Scranton, Pa.: ICS Intangibles Holding Co.): 45.*

[8] *Personal observations - J. Lindley. Information for drawing from Caring for Older Cats and Dogs, Robert Anderson and Barbara Wrede, (Charlotte, VT: Williamson Pub. Co. 1990): 47.*

2. THE CIRCULATORY SYSTEM

The circulatory system is the body's main transportation network. Its vehicle of choice is the liquid, blood. Via the flow of blood, oxygen, inhaled and absorbed at the lungs, is delivered to the body tissues and there, exchanged for carbon dioxide, to be returned to and exhaled by the lungs. The blood also carries nutrients (food) to, and wastes from, the cells. Locomotion for the blood is provided by a miraculous pump, the heart. The major parts of the circulatory system are: the heart, blood, the arterial system, the venous system and the spleen. The transport route, for oxygen, begins at the lungs. Blood picks up the oxygen, at the air sacs, by means of absorption (a sort of internal respiration, known as diffusion)[1] in the capillaries, the smallest of the network tubes. From there it goes to the heart (through the pulmonary vein) to be pumped out (through the aorta) to the body tissues, via the arterial system (arteries, arterioles and capillaries). At the cell level, oxygen is exchanged for carbon dioxide to be returned, through the venous system (capillaries, venules and veins) where it reenters the heart (through the vena cava) to be pumped back to the lungs.

Blood, sometimes called the River of Life, is the means of transportation of the cat's body essentials. To accomplish this, it is made up of red blood cells, to which the precious oxygen adheres. Besides the mode of transportation blood also provides two other services. It warms the cat's extremities and it contains disease fighters, the white blood cells. Blood is composed of red blood cells, white blood cells, platelets and plasma. Your cat, at maturity, has about 65 ml. (2.2 ounces) of blood per kilogram (2.2 pounds) of body weight. For, example, the body of a 12 pound cat would contain approximately 12 ounces of blood.[2]

The red blood cells, or erythrocytes, are actually yellowish, disc shaped cells, it is the iron-rich hemoglobin, they contain, that gives them their red color.[3] They are produced in the marrow of long bones. The items oxygen, carbon dioxide, nutrients and urea (a cellular waste) all bond with the red blood cells to be carried to and from the various parts of the cat's body. When a red blood cell becomes old (around 65-75 days)[4], it is taken to the spleen for removal. The spleen is a long flat organ located on the left side of the abdominal (stomach area) cavity. It is a special organ that also stores iron for hemoglobin production, emergency blood supply (in the event of an injury) and produces antibodies for the immune system.[5]

White blood cells also reside in the blood stream for quick transportation to injured or diseased, areas for bodily defense. They are called leukocytes and, although there are many forms with different names, they all serve the same function - to defend the cat's body against bacteria, disease and parasites. Neutrophils are the main disease fighters. Eosinophils and basophils fight in allergic reactions. Monocytes are larger cells that engulf and destroy bacteria, fungi and protozoas (parasites). Lymphocytes, the last type, help give the body immunity to diseases by producing antibodies. On the whole, they are a real group of warriors. When they die, during a battle, they become that pasty white substance, pus (most of us are familiar with), which is usually seen at an infection site. It is interesting that, while red blood cells may live up to 75 days, white blood cells live only about 12 hours.[6] That means the bone marrow, where they are also produced, must work overtime during an infection. Imagine that! Bones do a lot more than we give them credit for.

Platelets, or thrombocytes, are disc-shaped cells that also help in the event of an injury. In its normal state, blood is a liquid slightly thicker than water. When there is an injury, causing a break in a blood vessel, the network tubes, blood leaks out. A platelet, floating in the bloodstream, comes in contact with the injury site and attaches itself to it, attracting more platelets, to form a clump to plug, or clot, the leak of blood.

The last component of blood is plasma. Plasma comprises 60-70 percent of the blood.[7] It is a pale yellow liquid in which all the component cells float. It contains proteins, minerals and sugars. The protein part of plasma aids in disease fighting as well as clotting.

The primary organ of the circulatory system is the heart, the pumping system for the blood. The mature cat's heart is about the size of a small plum.[8] The heart is a structure, made up of muscle tissue, containing four chambers, through which the blood is pumped. The muscular layer is the myocardium. The four chambers are the left and right atria (upper) and the left and right ventricles (lower). The heart is lined by a serous (moisture emitting) membrane, the endocardium, and surrounded by another serous membrane, the pericardium. It is separated into two sides by a muscular wall, the septum. The flow of blood, being pumped through the heart, is regulated by valves (tricuspid and mitral) just like human hearts.

In a properly working heart, oxygenated blood is received, from the lungs, by the left atrium, pumped to the left ventricle, to be pumped out to the body tissues. Blood, containing carbon dioxide, arrives back at the heart where it enters the right atrium. It is then pumped into the right ventricle where it is pumped to the lungs to be re-oxygenated. The cat's pulse is a reflection of the heart pumping, or beating, and it can be located on the femoral artery inside the hind leg. A cat's heart normally beats anywhere from 120-240 times per minute, depending on exercise, stress, excitement or fever.[9]

The circulatory system is pretty much a mirror of the problems of the other systems. That is to say, it reflects what's wrong elsewhere. For example: 1. Due to the reduced oxygen output from the lungs, the respiratory system, the red blood cells will not carry enough oxygen to the cells. The result will be a bluish-gray color of the gums and tongue; 2. A poorly functioning urinary system may cause a buildup of urea in the blood. The gums may appear yellow in color. This can be the case of a malfunctioning kidney and the result will be anemia, seen as a decrease in the number of red blood cells, as well as a toxic buildup of urea, which will cause vomiting and diarrhea, in turn, resulting in an overall potassium loss - big trouble for an older cat. Anemia, itself, can be a frequent problem in older cats but once the cause is determined it can be treated. Potassium loss can be replaced with vitamins and food supplements.

When your cat seems ill your veterinarian will most likely do a blood test (known as a complete blood count or CBC) to check the number of red and white blood cells. He may also check if there is an abnormal amount of anything else in the bloodstream. By means of the test results, your veterinarian can form a better idea of what's happening to your sick baby. He can also give you an idea whether the problem is a normal breakdown, such as an aging spleen or kidney, or a disease, and which treatment is required.

Many of the diseases that can affect the circulatory system, the heart and blood, are congenital, present at time of birth, and have already surfaced and, hopefully, have been treated by the time your cat is middle-aged. There are, however, a few heart diseases that can develop during your cat's lifetime, called acquired heart diseases. They can be caused by a malfunctioning heart muscle, itself, or by a disease affecting another organ which may affect the heart beat rate, causing an arrhythmia. Arrhythmia is a change in the normal rate of heart beats.[10] It can be caused by oxygen deficiency to the heart, acid base imbalances, electrolyte imbalances, drugs, toxins and heart disease.[11] It usually results in decreased heart operation causing reduced flow of blood to the vital organs, the brain, spleen and kidneys. Your veterinarian will need to determine the cause of the arrhythmia and the required treatment.

The heart muscle is subject to several diseases that may affect middle-aged and older cats. They are known as cardiomyopathies. The most common type is hypertrophic cardiomyopathy, which predominately affects young to middle-aged male cats.[12] Another form is dilated cardiomyopathy which may occur in middle-aged to older cats.[13] This disease causes the heart muscle to become enlarged and at one time it was associated with the deficiency of taurine, a necessary mineral, in the cat's diet. It is my understanding that the cat food manufacturers have taken care of this by adequately raising the level of taurine in their products. In most cases, symptoms of heart disease will cause your cat to seem very tired and weak, with possible lack of appetite. Depending on which side of the heart muscle is involved the symptoms will vary. Labored and noisy breathing and fluid buildup in the lungs and abdominal cavity are also problem signs. Heart problems can be treated if discovered soon enough.

If your cat is diagnosed with a heart problem, do not get too depressed. According to Dr. James Ross, at the Department of Medicine at Tufts University School of Veterinary Medicine, "an animal can have heart disease and live a normal life for a number of years without acute symptoms or heart failure".[14] To repeat myself, early diagnosis and treatment is definitely advised.

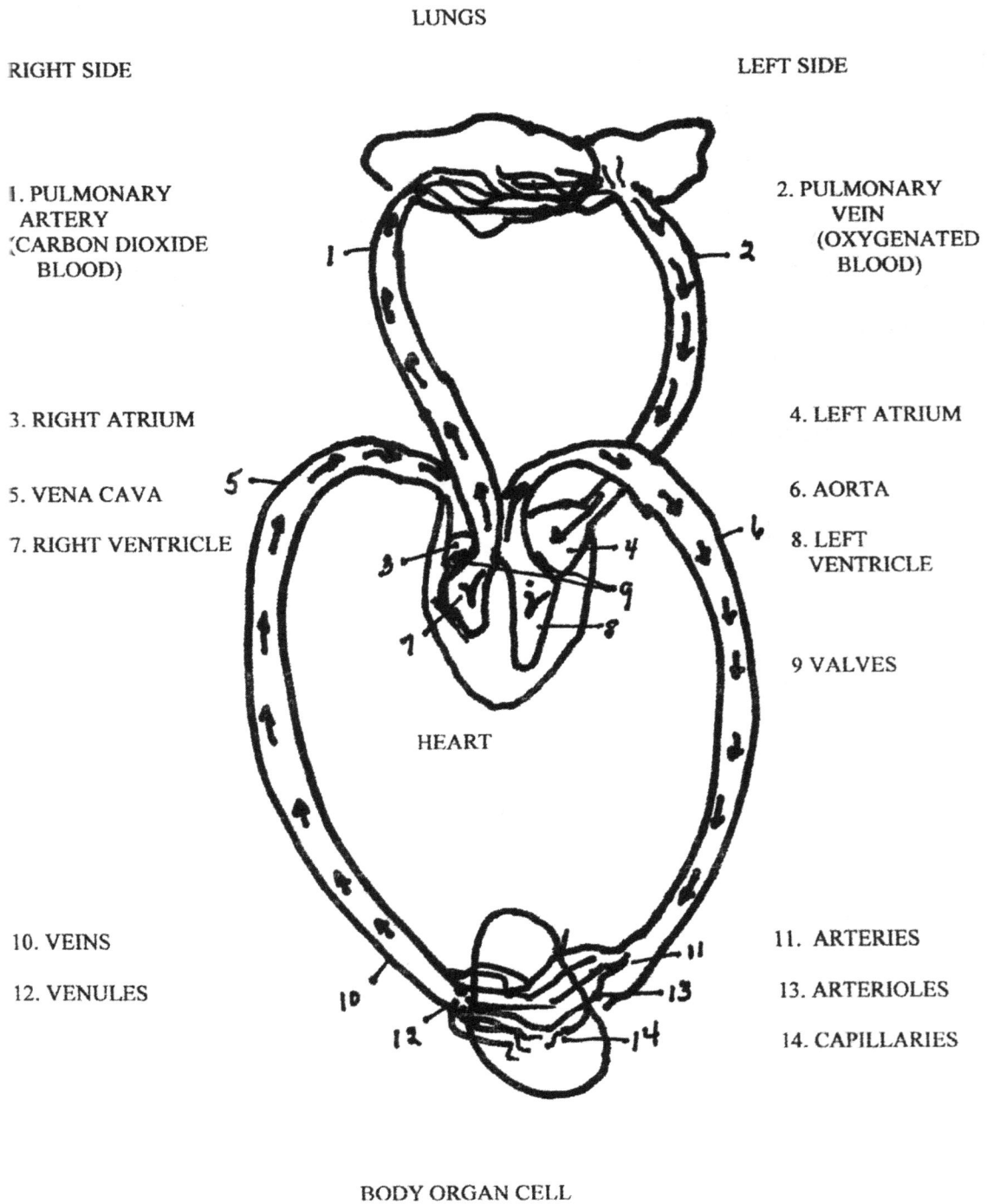

Judith Lindley

LUNGS

RIGHT SIDE

LEFT SIDE

1. PULMONARY
   ARTERY
   (CARBON DIOXIDE
   BLOOD)

2. PULMONARY
   VEIN
   (OXYGENATED
   BLOOD)

3. RIGHT ATRIUM

4. LEFT ATRIUM

5. VENA CAVA

6. AORTA

7. RIGHT VENTRICLE

8. LEFT
   VENTRICLE

9 VALVES

HEART

10. VEINS

12. VENULES

11. ARTERIES

13. ARTERIOLES

14. CAPILLARIES

BODY ORGAN CELL

THE CAT'S CIRCULATORY SYSTEM

78

NOTES

[1] *Anatomy and Physiology, Part I, Animal Science (Scranton, PA: ICS Intangibles Holding Co., 1994): 37.*

[2] *N. Sydney Moise, Circulatory System and Disorders, The Cornell Book of Cats (N.Y.: Villard Books div of Random House, 1992): 188.*

[3] *ibid.*

[4] *Anatomy and Physiology Part I, Animal Science (Scranton, P.A.: ICS Intangibles Holding Co., 1994): 28.*

[5] *ibid.*

[6] *ibid.*

[7] *N. Sydney Moise, Circulatory System and Disorders, The Cornell Book of Cats (N.Y.: Villard Books div of Random House, 1992): 189.*

[8] *ibid: 187.*

[9] *Same as 1 cited.*

[10] *N. Sydney Moise, Circulatory System and Disorders, The Cornell Book of Cats (N.Y.: Villard Books div of Random House, 1992): 191.*

[11] *bid.*

[12] *ibid: 192.*

[13] *ibid.*

[14] *James Ross, in "Feline Heart Disease", Catnip, a Newsletter of Tufts University School of Veterinary Medicine (January 1995): 5.*

3. THE DIGESTIVE SYSTEM

Without fuel for the engine the machine won't work. In this case the machine is your cat's body. Although oxygen is mandatory for life, your cat can't live on air alone. She also requires nourishment in the form of food and water. These nutrients are provided, for your cat, in the form of cat food. There are two important tricks for you; one to provide the proper food, and two, to convince your cat to eat the right amount of it. (The proper diet will be discussed in a later chapter.) Once you have provided the food and your cat eats it the process of digestion can begin.

Imagine the digestive system as a long canal (the alimentary canal) with the food being pushed along by waves (muscle contractions) into a pool (the stomach), after being mixed, and churned, around it enters the rapids (the small intestines) finally to be temporarily stored (the large intestine). All the while having the nutrients sucked out (absorbed), the water removed and then added to other waste waiting to be pushed out, at your cats convince, hopefully into a litter box. Of course it's a bit more complex than that.

The digestive system, also known as the digestive tract, is made up of the oral cavity (mouth, salivary glands, teeth and tongue), the back of the mouth (pharynx), the esophagus, stomach, small intestine and large intestine. Its function, the process of digestion, involves other organs, the liver and the pancreas. Its primary function is to breakdown nutrients, taken in as food and water, into usable materials to be absorbed and used by the body's cells, then prepare and dispose of the wastes. The digestive tract begins at the cat's mouth and ends at the cat's anus, with the actual digestive process occurring in the middle. Since the digestive system takes in the nutrients and processes them for use, any malfunctions here will cause problems elsewhere as well. A prime example of this is seen in older cats who are unattended and must fend for themselves. Due to poor diet and improper digestion they look worn and gaunt.

Digestion begins as soon as the cat takes the food in her mouth. As she tears and crushes it with her teeth, saliva, secreted by four pairs of salivary glands in the mouth,[1] is mixed in. Saliva contains an enzyme, ptyalin, which helps break down the starch in food. The saliva also lubricates the food into a bolus, or ball, for easy swallowing, and then the tongue passes the food back across the pharynx and into the esophagus. Swallowing begins as the tongue pushes food, into the opening, a wave of contraction forms, in the back of the mouth, to let go and propel the food down the esophagus to the stomach. When the food enters the stomach it is mixed with strong acid and powerful protein-digesting enzymes, produced by the stomach lining. The stomach contracts to mix the food and enzymes. After sufficient mixing, the food is propelled, by a wave of contraction, through the lower stomach opening, the pylorus, into the first part of the small intestine, the duodenum. There, the food is mixed with bile, from the liver, and pancreatic juices, from the pancreas. Bile salts, in the bile, break down and help absorb fats. Pancreatic juice neutralizes the stomach acid and, with powerful enzymes, breaks down complex proteins, fats and carbohydrates. From the duodenum the nutrients pass into the main portion of the small intestine, the jejunum, to be further reduced by enzymes and bile. When the food has been reduced as much as possible, by the small intestine, much of it is absorbed through the intestinal lining and transported, via the bloodstream, to the awaiting hungry cells. Whatever is not absorbed goes on into the large intestine, the colon. The large intestine absorbs water from the remaining food and further reduces it, producing a number of vitamins at the same time. This last part of breakdown is done by good (non-harmful) bacteria. There are as many as 100 billion bacteria, per gram of feces, in the large intestine.[2] These bacteria also aid in protection against disease.[3] After the large intestine has absorbed what's possible out of the remaining food, the rest becomes a waste and is stored, as fecal matter or feces, until it is eliminated, or voluntarily pushed out, by your cat, through the rectum and out the anus.

Upsets of the digestive system can be caused by many things. Beginning at the top, the mouth, the teeth age, become brittle and break, causing gums to become inflamed. Tartar and plaque can also cause inflamed gums. There are also changes in the secretions of the salivary glands. Aging animals can develop dry mouth, due to lack of saliva. However, I've noticed that many older cats have the opposite problem, drooling. The liver and pancreas age and slow down in enzyme production. There may also be a change in the muscle tone of the large intestine (colon) resulting in a change in bowel movements, specifically the consistency of feces.[4] What ever the change, the results are the same; vomiting, diarrhea and/or constipation.

There are two types of vomiting, regular vomiting, from the stomach and regurgitation, from the esophagus. Food brought up from the esophagus is only partially digested and still looks pretty much the same as when it was swallowed. It may also be tubular in shape. One cause of regurgitation is the cat gulping her food, which some older cats tend to do especially in a multi-cat household. Vomiting, from the stomach, can have more serious causes. I've noticed that older cats have a tendency toward food allergies. Some foods just don't agree with them so they'll eat grass, or groom excessively to ingest enough saliva to bring it all back up. Changing the diet may help. Hairballs will also cause your cat to vomit. Looking at the contents can give you a clue as to the cause. If vomiting becomes a chronic problem you need to consult your veterinarian for treatment.

Diarrhea can be a real problem for older cats. Not only is it messy and smelly to us imagine how the cat feels if it gets "stuck" all over. And, cleaning herself, what an awful taste that must be. No wonder cats become unthrifty. The most common cause of diarrhea, I've noticed in my older cats, has been due to food allergies. I try to avoid cat food that contains red and yellow dyes. I think the color may be added to cat food for our appeal rather than our cat's. More than often, the results of my feeding these foods, even for the sake of variety, has been the most colorful diarrhea. Needless to say, even though my older cats seem to like a bit of variety in their diet, I try not to do it too often. Temperature changes, particularly warm days and cold nights, as in the early seasons of spring and fall, cause my older cats to have diarrhea. I've noticed they drink more water, during this time, which probably adds to the watery consistency of their feces. They become more normal as they adjust to the temperature. PeptoBismol® can be given in small amounts, to soothe the stomach and calm the diarrhea. It is, however, a symptom reliever only, not a cure for the cause.

Constipation can be common in older cats. Along with the constipation they may also have lack of appetite, loss of weight and lack of energy.[5] Their feces become very hard and the cat will strain. Occasionally they will strain too hard and you may notice a little blood on the feces. Often hairballs can contribute to this. There are several types of hairball remedies, available over the counter, which contains a laxative to relieve the constipation. I've found that butter, licked off my finger, helps. If constipation becomes a chronic, painful problem for your cat you should see your veterinarian. There is a fairly new disorder, found in older cats, that is presently being researched. It is called idiopathic megacolon. It is an acquired disorder which causes the colon to become enlarged which results in ineffective transport of feces out of the cat's body. The result is severe and painful constipation. It is suggested that a smooth muscle disorder is the cause of it. The Morris Animal Foundation is presently funding Robert J. Washabau, VMD., PhD., at the University of Pennsylvania to research this problem.[6] The owners of afflicted cats report their pets to be in great discomfort. Please be on the lookout for this possibility in your older cat if she has chronic constipation.

There are a number of diseases, virus-type, which cause vomiting and diarrhea. Fortunately, if your cat has received regular vaccinations, she should be pretty much immune to them.

Intestinal parasites can be another problem entirely, although the resulting diarrhea, or vomiting, may be the same. The one-celled parasite giardiasis causes an older cat to have diarrhea and to also be unthrifty. She just doesn't feel quite right, so she doesn't wash. It is normal for your cat to wash herself many times during the day.[7] So when washing stops there is indeed something amiss. A cat with giardiasis may also have problems maintaining her weight. This can be a real problem for an older cat as so many of them get thinner with age anyway. Once your veterinarian has diagnosed giardiasis proper medication can be given. There is another parasite, a stomach worm, ollulanus tricuspis, that can cause chronic vomiting in adult cats.[8] The clue here is chronic. Anything that becomes chronic should be seen by your veterinarian for a specific diagnosis. Chronic vomiting and diarrhea can lead to severe dehydration. If your cat becomes too dehydrated the result could be fatal. I've been known to give my cats Pedialite® orally to combat dehydration.

Cancer can be a problem to the digestive system of old cats. Viruses, toxins or sometimes just age, itself, can change the growth of cells in the intestines.[9] This abnormal cell growth forms a tumor which, as it grows, causes a blockage. The blockage can cause intermittent bouts of vomiting and diarrhea that will worsen as the tumor grows. If discovered and diagnosed early it can be removed or treated.

The worst changes, I think, are the ones you can do absolutely nothing about. These changes are with the actual aging organ, the liver. The liver in an older cat is susceptible to cirrhosis, scarring and degeneration of the liver tissue. The liver tissue is replaced by scar tissue and cannot function properly. There is no cure for cirrhosis but there are special diets to slow it down. A failing liver can cause depression, lethargy, loss of appetite, increased thirst and urination, which also stresses the aging kidneys, occasional vomiting and diarrhea, sometimes neurologic dysfunction.[10] This is the point where personal decisions must be made to prevent suffering by your beloved friend. It is most important that any changes in your cat's normal bodily functions be checked right away.

One thing very consoling for me, a general rule of thumb taught to me by a very respected veterinarian:[11] "If it goes in one end OK and out the other end OK, don't worry about the middle."

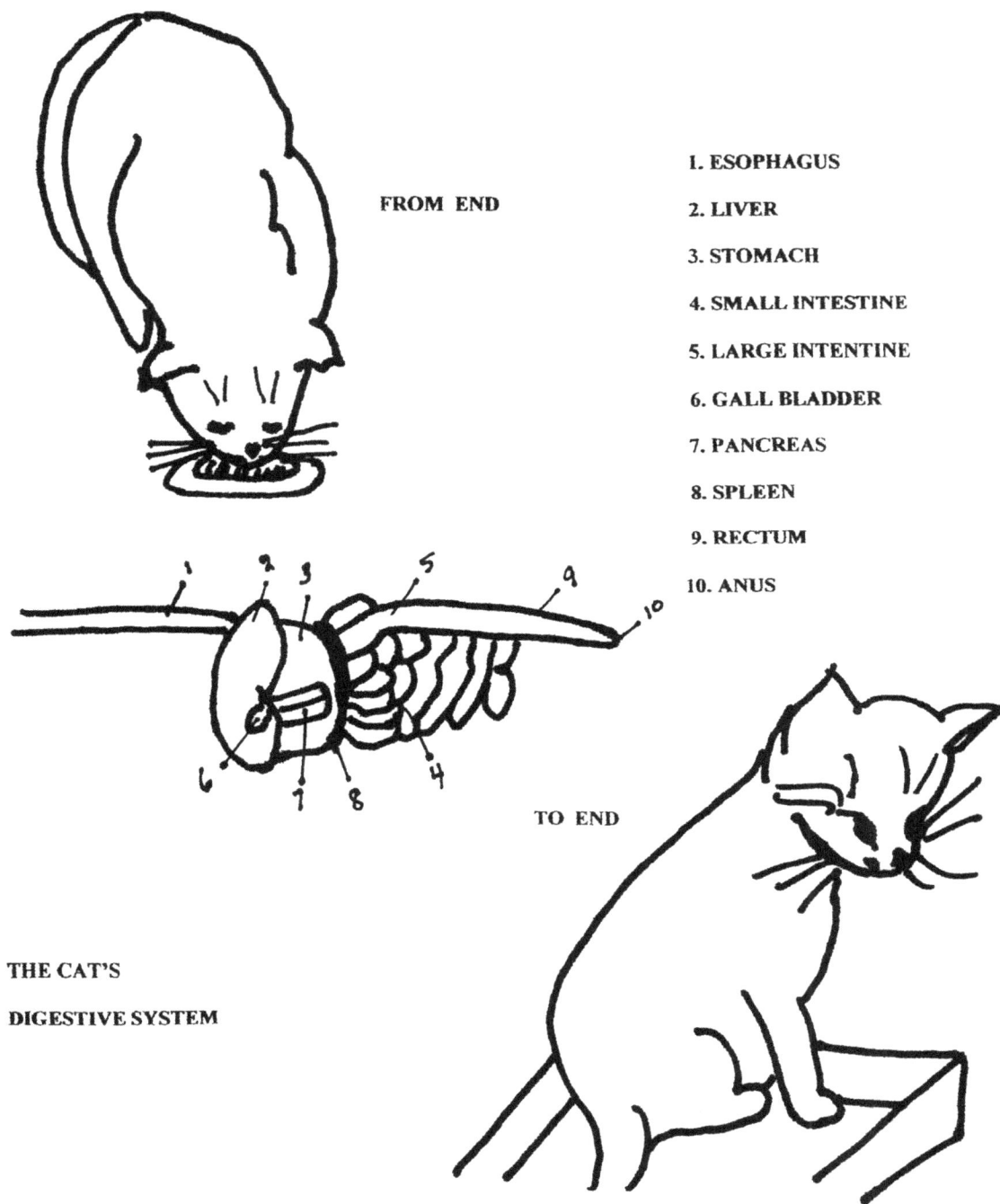

FROM END

1. ESOPHAGUS

2. LIVER

3. STOMACH

4. SMALL INTESTINE

5. LARGE INTENTINE

6. GALL BLADDER

7. PANCREAS

8. SPLEEN

9. RECTUM

10. ANUS

TO END

THE CAT'S

DIGESTIVE SYSTEM

NOTES

[1] *Roy V.H. Pollock, Digestive System and Disorders, The Cornell Book of Cats (N.Y.: Villard Books div of Random House, 1992): 226.*

[2] *ibid: 228.*

[3] *ibid.*

[4] *Michael S. Bodri, Animal Care: Prenatal Through Old Age, Animal Science, (Scranton, PA: ICS Intangibles Holding Co., 1994): 45.*

[5] *June Kirvan-Tuttle, Jeffrey E. Barlough, Mordecai Siegal and Leo A. Wuori, Aging Cats and Disorders, The Cornell Book of Cats (N.Y.: Villard Books div of Random House, 1992): 312. and Roy V.H. Pollock, Digestive System and Disorders, The Cornell Book of Cats (N.Y.: Villard Books, 1992): 235.*

[6] *Feline Constipation, Animal News of Morris Animal Foundation (Vol 11, 1995)*

[7] *Personal observations - J. Lindley.*

[8] *Same as 5 cited above: 233.*

[9] *Roy V.H. Pollock, Digestive System and Disorders, The Cornell Book of Cats, (N.Y.: Villard Books div of Random House, 1992): 234.*

[10] *ibid. also page 313 (liver disease, cirrhosis).*

[11] *Herman Salk, DVM, Palm Springs, Calif.*

4. THE URINARY SYSTEM

To pee or not to pee? That is the question.

It is very safe to say that anything taken in must eventually be let out, after the body has used as much of it as possible. The solid wastes pass out through the digestive tract, previously discussed. The liquid, absorbed by the intestinal lining, after being utilized, metabolized, by the body cells, returns to the bloodstream as waste to be carried to the kidneys, the beginning of the urinary system. The urinary system has two functions; it removes metabolic wastes from the body and regulates the chemical and water components of the blood,[1] by reabsorption and redistribution.

The urinary system is made up of two kidneys, two ureters (tubes connecting the kidneys to the bladder), one urinary bladder (a holding tank) and the urethra (the tube leading out of the body). The primary function of the urinary system is to remove liquid cellular wastes, made up mostly of urea and creatinine, from the cat's body before they build up and become toxic.[2] To do this the kidneys act as a marvelous filtering station, processing the wastes, then sending them, through the ureters, to the bladder, for storage, to be released, hopefully, into an awaiting litter box (if your cat is inside) or to the great outdoors.

The kidneys are located on each side of your cat's spine, just below the ribs.[3] They receive and filter the blood, removing water and fluids, for recycling (on an as needed basis) or excretion, and urea, as well as creatinine, to be excreted before they poison your cat. The kidneys maintain the balance of necessary electrolytes, sodium, potassium and chloride, and they regulate the level of acidity in your cat's body. Blood enters the kidneys, through the renal artery, and then flows through smaller arteries until it reaches the kidney's nephrons. Each kidney is made up of about 200,000 nephrons.[4] Each nephron is made up of a mass of blood vessels called: a glomerulus; a proximal tubule; the loop of Henle; a distal tubule and a collecting duct. The blood enters the glomerulus, is filtered, separating the fluid from the cells, then passes into the proximal tubule, where needed substances are reabsorbed for recycling through the body. From the proximal tubule the remaining fluid, now known as urine, goes through the loop of Henle, into the distal tubule and the collecting duct, where more fluid is reabsorbed. From there the urine passes into the renal pelvis and out through the ureters to the bladder. A great filtering job and hopefully a job well done.

Normal water intake, for your cat, should be about one cup per five pounds of body weight per day (with adjustments for amount of exercise and temperature).[5] Urine output should be about two cups per five pounds of body weight per day.[6] The extra amount takes in account the water absorbed from all solids as well as any regular water taken in. Too much deviation from this is considered abnormal and should be checked. When your cat drinks too much water, it is known as polydipsia. If she urinates too frequently, it is known as polyuria. Polyuria sometimes causes your cat to urinate in places other than her litter box.

As your cat ages, you may notice a decline in the normal function of the kidneys. Over time the kidneys will not be able to concentrate urine (remove enough water for reabsorption) which results in a larger amount of more diluted urine. The waste products aren't filtered out as well and toxins may build up. In other words, your cat's kidneys begin to wear out and fail. Kidney failure is life threatening.[7] The most common cause of kidney damage in the older cat, chronic interstitial nephritis (CIN), is a destruction of nephron tissue, within the kidneys, causing scarring and shriveling. CIN can lead to dangerous dehydration followed by constipation. Overall warning signs are weight loss, dehydration, increased urination, increased thirst, poor appetite, bad breath, mouth ulcers and occasional vomiting.[8] Chronic kidney disease needs to be carefully monitored by you and your cat's veterinarian. The veterinarian may want to run a blood test, called a BUN (for blood, urea and nitrogen levels), to check your cat's progress. Fortunately there are special diets that can help your cat adjust to her condition.

To help your cat with an aging urinary system, first, have plenty of fresh water available at all times and second, watch for any changes that might require a trip to the veterinarian. With necessary medication and proper diet, as prescribed by your veterinarian, your aging cat may still live contented and comfortable in the autumn of her life.

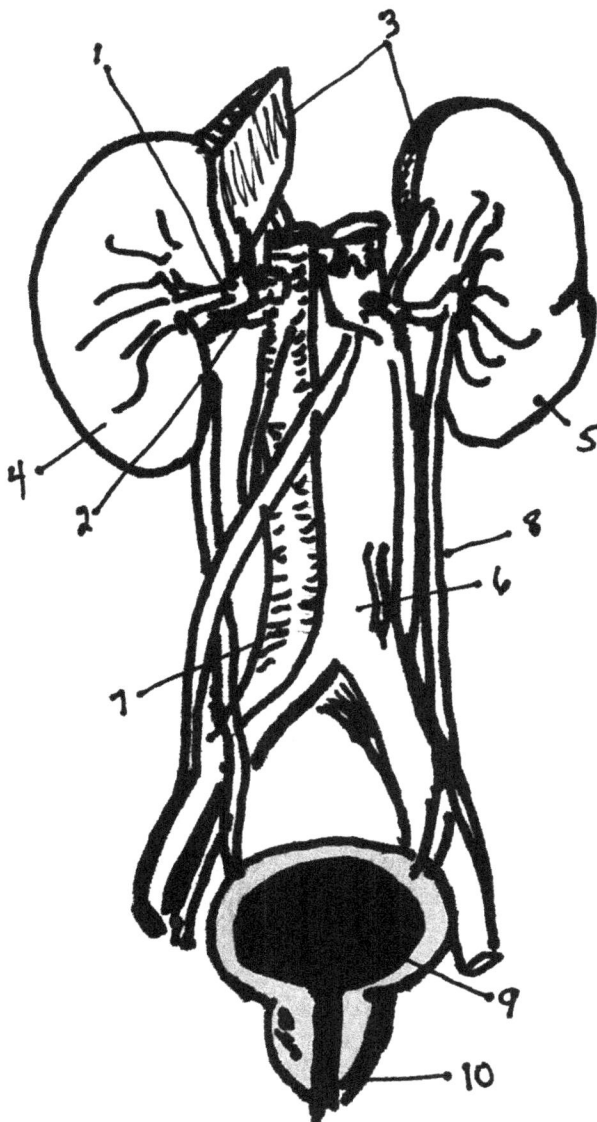

1. RENAL ARTERY

2. RENAL VEIN

3. ADRENAL GLANDS

4. RIGHT KIDNEY

5. LEFT KIDNEY

6. AORTA

7. INFERIOR VENA CAVA

8. URETER

9. BLADDER

10. URETHRA

THE CAT'S URINARY TRACT

Judith Lindley

NOTES

1 *Johnny D. Hoskins and June Kirvan-Tuttle, Urinary System and Disorders, The Cornell Book of Cats (N.Y.: Villard Books div of Random House 1992): 206*

2 *ibid.*

3 *"The Filtering Station of the Body", Catnip, a Newsletter of Tufts University School of Veterinary Medicine (September, 1995): 3.*

4 *ibid.*

5 *Ilana Reisner, Special Report, Cornell's Animal Health Newsletter, (August 1994): 3.*

6 *ibid.*

7 *Michael S. Bodri, Animal Care: Prenatal Through Old Age, Animal Science, (Scranton, P.A.: ICS Intangibles Holding Co., 1994): 45.*

8 *June Kirvan-Tuttle, Jeffrey E. Barlough, Mordecai Siegal and Leo A. Wuori, Aging Cats and Disorders, The Cornell Book of Cats (N.Y.: Villard Books div of Random House, 1992): 311.*

90

5. THE NERVOUS SYSTEM

A common saying: "Nervous as a cat", says much. It is well known that cats are high-strung and super sensitive creatures. It's really no wonder, though, when you think about how sensitive their other senses are, of course they would have to have a delicate, but quick, nervous system.

(Welcome to the wonderful system of nerves. Your tour guide, through this system, is Ned, one of our head neurons. Transportation is provided you by the red corpuscles (via their bloodstream)…")

The ultimate control of the cat's body, the brain, coordinates the other systems through the spinal cord and a complex network of peripheral nerves.[1] Imagine your cat's brain as a major control room, receiving messages and relaying an appropriate response. There is one thing you must remember, in the case of an older cat, the response may not be quite as quick, as when she was younger. Sometimes, aging muscles and bones just don't move as fast anymore.

("You notice those strange flashes on your right? Those are messages, relaying from one nerve to another, going to, or from, our major control room, the brain…")

When you think of your cat's body covered with her lovely fur coat (Sphynx excepted), consider this, each hair is connected to a nerve ending. So, each hair is capable of sensing a change and relaying a message to the brain. Therefore, your cat really is a bundle of nerves. No wonder cats are so sensitive and high strung. Even a small wisp of air can cause their hairs to stir. Combine that with vibration of the floor under your footsteps, and your cat really becomes alive and alert, even when awakened from a deep sleep.

("It's almost 6 am now and our host, the cat, is curled up still. What's that? A brilliant flash coming in from the ears. Must be breakfast on the way….")

It's always said, "my cat comes to the opening of a can." Your cat hears the can opening, the sound vibrations travel through the ears, exciting the auditory nerve, which in turn, signals the brain that something is heard. The brain interprets the noise as the can opener. Having heard this particular sound before, a signal occurs. The brain gets excited and sends out all sorts of messages. Signals sent to the eyes (through the optic nerve) to look for the locale of the noise and to the muscles to move in the proper direction, and so on. It is a little more complex than simply running across the floor. To make this can opening sequence even more complex add to it the other sense, the nose. Your cat inhales the aroma of the food being prepared. The nose is stimulated by the aroma; the olfactory receptors relay the 'smell' to the brain. The brain categorizes it, selects the closest memory. "Ah! I've smelled this before." The brain sends a message to the mouth, "This food is great! Please, salivate to enjoy this more." Your cat can now hardly wait to be served. And, if your cat arrives before the food is ready, she will circle, meowing in frustration. This brings into play all kinds of nerves, including ours.

The nervous system can be divided into two interconnected parts, the central nervous system (brain and spinal cord) and the peripheral nervous system (cranial, spinal and peripheral nerves). Each nerve is called a neuron. Each neuron is a body cell, with a nucleus and cytoplasm, similar to all other body cells. But nerve cells have branches (dendrites) and fingers (axons) protruding from them. The dendrites act as receptors and the axons are the transmitters.[2] One neuron is connected to an adjacent neuron at a site called a synapse. The signals are actually electrical impulses that cross from one neuron to another.

There are two forms of control of the nervous system. One, voluntary, mostly seen as a movement, or motor response. The signal, from the brain, travels down the spinal cord, through the peripheral nerves to the appropriate muscle(s) to make your cat move, such as, running to the sound of the can opener. Two, involuntary, for example the digestive tract, moving the food along, or the beating of her heart. The involuntary or autonomic nervous system also has two parts, the parasympathetic and the sympathetic nervous system. These two systems alternate with each other. The parasympathetic nervous system operates when the cat is normally unstressed. The sympathetic nervous system takes over, when the cat becomes stressed, to increase heart beat, dilate eyes and increase blood supply to the muscles.[3]

("and over here... oh, oh, there's an intermittent flashing in the vicinity of the spine. Must be trouble ahead. Please check your seat belts.")

Most problems, disorders, occurring with the nervous system are attributed to injuries, from auto encounters, or falls. Good news, however, according to Cornell's Feline Health Center, this affects "less than 1 per cent of the feline population".[4] The bad news is that older cats seem to be prone to falls. So, when you find your babies staring at the counter top, from the floor, it's best to gently lift them up to avoid a possible fall. Remember, it's not just the fall that is bad, it's that abrupt landing. If an older cat lands improperly she may slip a disc which could put pressure on the spinal cord, causing inflammation and even paralysis, in severe cases.

The scariest thing I've seen in my older cats is nervous seizures. Seizures can be a result of many causes, so it's best to check with your cat's veterinarian if they happen more than once. The seizures I've seen have been related to failing liver and/or kidneys. Signs of seizure were glassy eyes, violent meowing, tail thrashing, staggering, falling on one side, trembling, leg paddling and sometimes uncontrolled urinating. After the seizure subsided my cats slowly sat up, looked around, and seemed a little confused. Fortunately, I've only seen this, four or five times. Thank God for that because there was nothing I could do for them, short of making sure they didn't hurt themselves while it was happening. Afterwards I called the veterinarian for an appointment and took them in to be examined.

Older cats can also be affected with a problem similar to that of older humans - a stroke. It is called feline ischemic encephalopathy. It is the result of sudden deprivation of the blood supply to part of the cat's brain. Symptoms are depression, circling, incoordination, or seizures.[5] It may leave the cat with some problems such as a change in behavior, sight or some neurologic (nervous) function.[6]

Occasionally an older cat will exhibit signs of senility. This hasn't happened in my cats too often. Once in awhile I hear one crying at night, wandering in the hall, and seem to be confused when I approach her. I also catch some of them staring at nothing in a corner. In my opinion, these would be the most noticeable signs of senility. Nightly wandering and confusion can be attributed to the decrease of oxygen supply to the brain, something that naturally occurs with age.[7] It is interesting to note that the brain can also shrink a little with age. This shrinking is caused by a gradual degeneration of brain tissue and signs include incoordination, confusion and lethargy.[8] Since we all must age, senility is something we can do little about. As I researched to update this revised edition, I came across more recent information on senility. It is now called feline cognitive dysfunction. Symptoms, of this disorder, include: staring at walls; night wandering; yowling or vocalizing at night; irritability; confusion and disorientation (which may lead to inappropriate use of the litter box). Pretty much covers everything. Research is being done to find causes, other than normal aging, for this condition.[9]

On the brighter side, one of the most beautiful sounds I've ever heard is due, in part, to a nervous response, voluntary or involuntary; I'm not sure which. But I am sure it's the most comforting sound - the most magical whisper, that only a cat can possess - the purr.

("Thank you for taking our tour of the nervous system. Please remain seated until we come to a complete stop.")

NOTES

1 *Brian A. Summers and Jeffrey E. Barlough, Nervous System and Disorders, The Cornell Book of Cats (N.Y.: Villard Books div of Random House, 1992): 213.*

2 *ibid: 212.*

3 *"The Nervous System: The Information Super Highway", Catnip, a Newsletter of Tufts University Sch. of Vet. Med, (October 1995): 5.*

4 *Same as 1 cited above.*

5 *ibid: 216.*

6 *ibid.*

7 *Michael S. Bodri, Animal Care: Prenatal Through Old Age, Animal Science (Scranton, PA: ICS Intangibles Holding Co., 1994): 45.*

8 *June Kirvan-Tuttle, Jeffrey B. Barlough, Mordecai Siegal and Leo A. Wuori, Aging Cats and Disorders, The Cornell Book of Cats (N.Y.: Villard Books div of Random House, 1992): 313.*

9 *Dr. Borns-Weil, In Extra Care for the Senior Cat, Catnip, Cummings School of Veterinary Medicine at Tufts University. (March 2018): 6.*

6. THE ENDOCRINE SYSTEM

Influence is the power to affect others, ie. the power to produce effects because of position, ability and wealth.[1]

The endocrine system is the one system that has the most influence, or control, over all the cat's body systems. It is made up of a number of glands. The power behind their influence is their position, in relation to the other body organs, their ability to produce specialized secretions, hormones, and their wealth in the abundance of these secretions. Their secret of influence is in their construction. They have no ducts, (tubes leading to other organs) and are therefore known as ductless glands. Being ductless, they release their secretions directly into the bloodstream. The secretions then travel to their site of effect.

The glands of your cat's endocrine system are the thyroid, parathyroids, adrenals, pancreas, gonads and the pituitary. The thyroid is made up of two lobes and folds partially around the trachea. The parathyroids are four small glands, in two pairs, located, one pair each, on each lobe of the thyroid. The adrenals are adjacent to each kidney. The pancreas is located near the liver. The gonads are your cat's reproductive organs, testes (male) and ovaries (female). The pituitary is located at the base of the brain.

Each gland, or set of glands, influences your cat's body in a different way, but the Master of Control is the pituitary gland. It releases special hormones that, in turn, affect the hormonal secretions of all the other glands, with the exception of the pancreas. (See Chart) To better understand how this works, imagine the pituitary gland as a tiny engineer (I'll call him Ed) monitoring a control panel. On the panel are levers for each gland. Ed carefully monitors the production level, or output, of each gland and moves the levers accordingly. Ed, himself, is regulated by the hypothalamus, part of the brain (the big boss), which controls his output.[2]

The endocrine system works something like this:

From birth to four years old the primary output will be, from the pituitary gland itself, the growth hormone (GH). This is followed by, beginning around five months old, the reproductive hormones. The growth hormone begins to wane around three years but by that time the reproductive hormones are in full swing. Ed is raising the levers for the gonads while lowering his GH lever.

Hopefully, since you are obviously reading this with an older cat in mind, you have already been through the reproductive delights. But, in case you haven't, there are a few things that need be said. As the levels of hormones surge through their systems the males, known also as tom cats and studs, can become unmanageable. They become urine sprayers, marking everything, and anything, close as their territory. Then they become restless and roam, looking for new females, subsequently fighting for attention. The females, known also as queens, if unrestricted, will begin producing litter after litter. Removal of the gonads, neutering and spaying, prevents many problems, both for you and for the health and safety of your cat. Five to six months seems to be all right for spaying females, but seven months may be a better time to neuter males.[3] If you are a breeder, trying to perfect a specific breed, then you should consider retiring your cat somewhere around six years old. By that time all appropriate ribbons should have been acquired and all the offspring reared. Diseases of the reproductive system of intact females can be devastating for both you and your cat. According to Cornell University, mammary tumors comprise between six and eleven percent of all feline cancers, and they tend to occur in older cats.[4] Like all tumors they will need to be surgically removed. The worst problem is a disorder of the uterus called pyometritis. It is an accumulation of pus and debris retained in the uterus. Its frequency increases with age and it can be fatal.[5] It's best to avoid these complications in your cat's life, by having your cat spayed early.

Fortunately for Ed, our controller, around four to six years the gonadal hormones should begin to slow down a bit. He should be able to take a coffee break.

At eight years old the thyroid lever begins to move a bit. This may be an indication of approaching problems. Suddenly, at nine years old, Ed loses his ability to control the thyroid gland, as the lever is jerked from his hand and the output skyrockets. An alarm sounds as hyperthyroidism sets in.

Between the ages of eight and ten it's like an emotional bomb goes off. Cats of this age seem to be touchy and easily traumatized, particularly by changes in their environment, or surroundings, i.e. a move or abandonment.[6] If problems are going to develop, they seem to do so at this time. According to Cornell University, the most common endocrine disorder in older cats is hyperthyroidism.[7] It is not yet known whether hyperthyroidism is the result of a primary thyroid disorder or if an external factor, i.e. nutrition or environment, is responsible for the overactive thyroid gland.[8] What happens to your cat is the over production of the thyroid hormone speeds up her heart, causing the body to require more food, but the hyperactivity keeps her thin, even though she's eating more. She will eat faster and may vomit because of too much air intake when gulping. Signs to watch for are weight loss, increased appetite, hyperactivity, restlessness, increased thirst and urination, vomiting, diarrhea, muscle weakness, stronger and rapid heart beat, and of course since she isn't feeling up to par, a dull and unkempt coat. Should you see any of these signs, please see your veterinarian. Once diagnosed, medication, or treatment, can be given to stabilize her thyroid levels, or if necessary the thyroid gland may be surgically removed.

At the control panel, Ed is now able to control the thyroid lever. However, now to his amazement, the pancreas lever, for insulin output, is lowering. This lever is separate and not under his control. He watches, helplessly, as the lever lowers. Your cat begins to show signs of diabetes mellitus.

Diabetes mellitus is a disease of middle-aged and older cats. Although it can strike at any age, it is most commonly seen in cats of eight years and older. Strangely, it occurs more commonly in male than in female cats.[9] Also, overweight cats seem to be more at risk.[10] Diabetes mellitus is the result of a lack of insulin which causes the body to be unable to properly utilize blood sugar. The unused sugar is added to the urine resulting in an increased volume of urine, and frequent urination. Signs will be increased thirst and urination, followed by lethargy, increased appetite, weight loss, rear leg weakness, diarrhea, vomiting, and lastly, loss of appetite. Your cat may start out overweight then thin rapidly. Other signs may include thinning or loss of hair coat, chronic bladder disease and sore or inflamed tongue and gums.[11] It is very important to see your veterinarian if you see any of these symptoms. Diabetes mellitus, when diagnosed early, can be treated but it involves owner education. Insulin injections may be given on a regular schedule. All needs must be discussed with your veterinarian.

Other diseases associated with the aging endocrine system are hypothyroidism (the under production of thyroid), hypo- or hyperadrenocorticism, but they are not nearly as common as hyperthyroidism and diabetes mellitus.

Hopefully none of these problems will happen to your cat and her Ed will be able to maintain control of all the levers for proper hormonal output. Of course, not all cats will have these problems but it's always best to be prepared. The best thing you can do for your cat is to provide a good diet and, sometime around ten years old, take her to your veterinarian for a complete check up, including a blood test. This will give you the opportunity to discuss any possible upcoming problems. The visit will also give you peace of mind and assurance that Ed is on the job for your cat.

Gland	Produces	Effects	Problems
1. THYROID	Thyroine (T4) and tri-iodothyronine (T3)	regulates overall metabolism (how the body uses it's fuel)	HYPERTHYROIDISM Hypothyroidism (rare)
2. PARATHYROIDS	Parathyroid hormone (PTH)	controls use of calcium and Phosphorous	
3. ADRENALS	from the outer region: (the cortex) steroids; the corticosteroids (cortisol and corticosterone)	elevates blood sugar, increase fat and protein breakdown	hypo- and hyper-adrenalcorticism
	oldosterone	controls sodium chloride and potassium balance	
	glucorticoids	use of carbohydrates fats and protiens	
	mineralocorticoids	balance of electrolytes and water	
	from the middle: (the medulla) epinephrine also known as adrenaline	elevates blood sugars and increases blood pressure and heart output	
4. PANCREAS	insulin	regulates the use of blood sugar	DIABETES MELLITUS

Gland	Produces	Effects	Problems
5. GONADS			
testes	testosterone	reproduction and fertility	
ovaries	progesterone estrogen		
6. PITUITARY THE MASTER CONTROL	adrenocorticotropic hormone (ACTH)	controls adrenal cortex	
	thyroid stimulating hormone (TSH)	controls the thyroid gland's production of T_4 and T_3	
	follicle-stimulating hormone (FSH)	growth of ovarian follicles, production of sperm	
	luteinzing hormone (LH)	stimulates the testes to secrete testosterone and the ovaries to produce estrogen and progesterone	
	growth hormone (GH)	controls growth rate	

Based on information from:
Cornell's Book of Cats, Endocrine System
Chapter 27 pages 243-244

NOTES

[1] *Influence, Webster's New World Dictionary (N.Y.: Warner Books Inc, 1990): 304.*

[2] *Hypothalamus, Anatomy and Physiology: Part 2, Animal Science, (Scranton, PA.: ICS Intangibles Holding Co., 1994): 33 & 34.*

[3] *Personal observation - J. Lindley.*

[4] *Donald Lein, Reproductive Disorders, The Cornell Book of Cats (N.Y.: Villard Books div of Random House, 1992): 112.*

[5] *ibid: 113.*

[6] *Personal observations - J. Lindley.*

[7] *June Kirvan-Tuttle, Jeffrey E. Barlough, Mordecai Siegal and Leo A. Wuori, Aging Cats and Disorders, The Cornell Book of Cats, (N.Y.: Villard Books div of Random House, 1992): 312.*

[8] *Jeffrey E. Barlough, June Kirvan-Tuttle, Leo A. Wuori, Endocrine System and Metabolic Disorders, The Cornell Book of Cats (N.Y.: Villard Books div of Random House, 1992): 422.*

[9] *Feline Diabetes, Catnip, a Newsletter of Tufts University, School of Veterinary Medicine (July 1994): 4.*

[10] *ibid.*

[11] *Jeffrey E. Barlough, June Kirvan-Tuttle, Leo A. Wuori, Endocrine System and Metabolic Disorders, The Cornell Book of Cats (N.Y.: Villard Books div of Random House, 1992): 246.*

7. THE IMMUNE SYSTEM

"The hair says there's an invader approaching. If it penetrates our first line of defense (the skin) we will have to mobilize and fight.", Sergeant of Immune System Forces.

The immune system is made up of a multitude of components that work together to protect your cat from invading micro-organisms. The tissues and organs of the immune system can be grouped into two categories: primary lymphoid organs and secondary lymphoid organs. The primary lymphoid organs are those responsible for production of lymphocytes (the response cells), the bone marrow, thymus and mucosal-associated lymphoid tissue (MALT). The secondary lymphoid organs are those that trap, by means of filtering, the invaders where they can be destroyed, the lymph nodes, spleen, and portions of the bone marrow and MALT.[1]

The immune system is what protects your cat from bacterial and viral infections by providing antibodies which aid in fighting them off. It works in conjunction with the leukocytes, the white blood cells, and together the invaders are not only destroyed, by the leukocytes, but the immune system provides protection against future assaults.

When your cat was a youngster, sometime around four to six weeks old, she should have received the first set of vaccinations. These vaccinations, usually given in two sets, are for dangerous, highly contagious, diseases such as cat fever (panleukopenia), upper respiratory diseases (rhinotracheitis) and cat flu (calicivirus) and similar viruses. These are then followed by yearly boosters. These vaccines are a small dose of live, dead or modified (weakened) viruses that are strong enough to cause an immune response, but not make your cat sick. What happens is the immune system receives a signal of the invading virus and sends a message, through the lymph, to produce antibodies. The antibodies attach themselves to the invader, which signals the white cells that there are invaders, and to come and destroy them. Stimulation of these antibodies, on a regular basis, protects your cat in the event she closely contacts a cat with the disease. [2]

During normal times, times of peace, the immune system monitors your cat's systems. Lymphocytes and monocytes (the response cells) and lymphokines, messenger molecules, float in the lymph system. The lymph system is a network of vessels that transport a fluid, lymph, from body tissues back into the circulatory system. It is designed to help drain tissues by removing large wastes that can't otherwise be handled by the blood vessels.[3] These wastes are filtered by lymph nodes.

When an invasion is imminent the lymphocytes and monocytes respond and a message, through the lymphokines, is sent to the bone marrow to produce white blood cells to destroy the invader. These white blood cells are specifically designed to fight the invader. Macrophages are best suited to take care of bacteria, fungi, viruses, parasites, toxins and altered body cells. Once the invader has been immobilized, or engulfed, the macrophages signal local lymphocytes (T-cell lymphocytes), to mount an attack, an immune response, against it.[4] The thymus, an organ in your cat's chest, regulates the growth of these special lymphocytes, the T-cells, which assist in production of antibodies. Other white blood cells, neutrophils, come to fight as well but they are not capable of directing the help of the lymphocytes. However, they are especially helpful in battles involving foreign material, like bacteria.

Once the battle is over the destroyed white cells, along with other cellular debris, including the dead invaders, are carried to the lymph nodes. You may feel the lymph nodes in your cat, under her front legs and under her chin, when they are swollen. The lymph nodes filter the lymph and hold the invaders so that the immune system can have a better look at them and create an appropriate antibody for future protection, should the invader's relatives choose to come. The remainder of the destroyed cells, dead red blood cells included, and foreign material are taken to the spleen for filtering and removal.

In the aging cat the immune system does not operate at full potential,[5] and the sinus membranes seem to become more sensitive, as well. This can be seen as mild allergies, which may increase with age. My older cats seem to have more problems in the winter, with sneezing and sniffles. This may be an allergic reaction to moisture.[6] Other times of the year some of them develop allergies to pollen, resulting in watering eyes and skin lesions, such as hives or hot spots.

True allergies are the result of a slow, or inappropriate, response, of the immune system, to relatively innocuous antigens, such as house-dust mites, pollen and dander.[7] Other allergies can develop, particularly sensitivity to foods containing certain dyes. As I mentioned in the chapter on the digestive system, I try to avoid foods containing red and yellow dyes. I've just recently experienced patchy coat in six of my cats due to feeding a food not regularly their normal diet. As soon as I went back to their regular food the problem disappeared.

The absolutely worst drain on the cat's immune system is stress. When a cat is under stress she becomes over excited, or, the exact opposite, depressed and withdrawn. This causes the immune system to go into a sort of shock and slow down. This shock allows the cat to be open to antigens and she can easily become sick. Stress can be caused by many things but, in the cat, it is mostly due to changes, especially changes in her environment. As she adjusts to the change she will become more normal and her immune system should resume proper operation. Sometimes during times of stress, vitamin supplements are needed so see your veterinarian. Talk to your veterinarian about vitamin B complex with Vitamin C.

It's important to watch your older cat for signs of allergies. If your cat's immune system is operating properly there should be no problems. Remember, all the body systems slow down with age. Keep them warm and comfortable, keep stress to a minimum, and you should have relatively little, if any, problems.

NOTES

1 *Jeffrey E. Barlough, Immune System and Disorders, The Cornell Book of Cats (N.Y.: Villard Books div. of Random House, 1992): 250.*

2 *ibid.*

3 *The Lymphatic System, Anatomy and Physiology, Part I, Animal Science (Scranton, P.A: ICS Intangibles Holdings Co., 1994): 28.*

4 *N. Sydney Moise, Circulatory System and Disorders, The Cornell Book of Cats (N.Y.: Villard Books div of Random House, 1992: 189.*

5 *Michael S. Bodri, Animal Care: Prenatal Through Old Age, Animal Science (Scranton, P.A: ICS Intangibles Holding Co, 1994): 43-44.*

6 *Personal observation - J. Lindley.*

7 *Jeffrey E. Barlough, Immune System and Disorders, The Cornell Book of Cats (N.Y.: Villard Books div of Random House, 1992): 252.*

Whether your cat is 16 years old, like Martha Jane (right) or 26 years old, like Miranda (below) seniors are sensational.

Martha Jane shares her home with Amy and Buddy Andrews in New Albany, Mississippi.

Miranda shares her home with Trudy Thomas in Newport Beach, California.

The following pages are photos of senior cats. They are living proof that there's definitely life after 10 years.

Cat: Henry age 14
Owner/Photo: Leah & Taz White of
Fairfield, California

Cat: Logan age 14
Cwner/Photo: Leah & Taz White of
Fairfield, California

Cat: Agatha age 18
Owner/Photo: J. Lindley of
Morongo Valley, California

Cat: Edwin K. Cat age 10

Owner/Photo: Samantha Adams

of Palm Desert, California

Cat: Thomas age 12

Owner/Photo: Susan Livingston

of North Carolina

Cat: Callie age 19

Owner/Photo: Teresa Hemphill of

Hawthorne, California

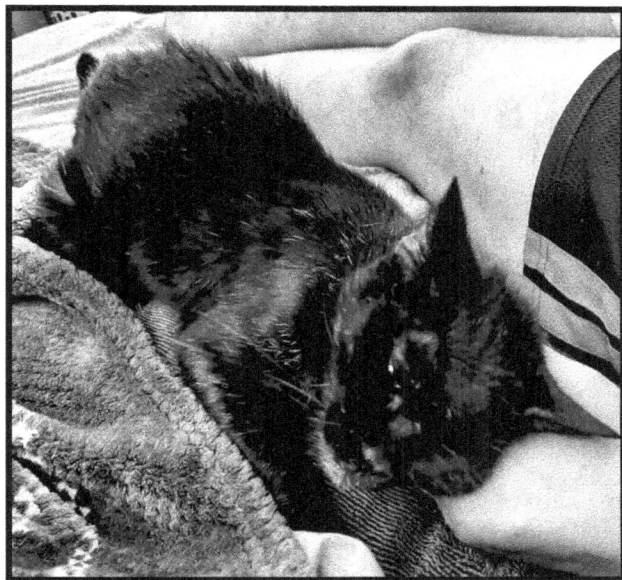

Cat: Lola age 13
Owner/Photo: Alexandra Ortega
of Palm Desert, California

Cat: Ninja age 11
Owner/Photo: Alexandra Ortega
of Palm Desert, California

Cat: Lady Gray age 22
Owner/Photo: Betty Pierce of
Huntington Beach, California

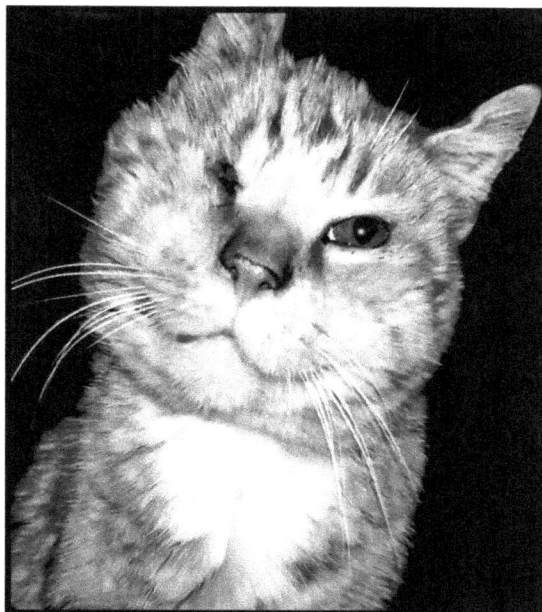

Cat: Red Man age 29

Owner/Photo: Jaynee Calon of Duncansville,
Pennsylvania

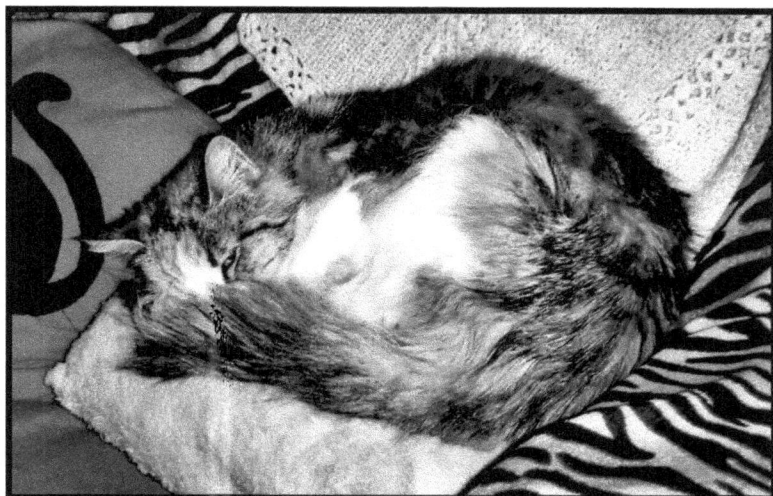

Cat: Callie age 20

Owner/Photo: J. Lindley of
Morongo Valley, California

Cat: Rory age 20

Owner: Bridget Moore
of Missoula, Montana

Photo: Patricia Hall

Cat: Abby age 18
Owner/Photo: J. Lindley of
Morongo Valley, California

Cat: Lily age 10
Owner/Photo: Cassandra Gess of
Myrtle Beach, South Carolina

Cat: Mary Jane age 12
Owner/Photo: Cassandra Gess of
Myrtle Beach, South Carolina
(the cover cat)

Cat: Holly age 12
Owner/Photo: Clare Earthey of
Chalfont St Giles, in
Buckinghamshire UK

Cat: Huck age 14
Owner/Photo: Clare Earthey of Chalfont
St Giles, in Buckinghamshire UK

Cat: Patches age 22
Owner/Photo: J. Lindley of
Morongo Valley, California

113

Cat: Suki age 13
Owner: Maurine Cecil of
Signal Hill, California
Photo: Jaime Rea

Cat: Sadie age 13
Owner: Maurine Cecil of
Signal Hill, California
Photo: Jaime Rea

Cat: Mo age 20
Owner/Photo: J. Lindley of
Morongo Valley, California

Cat: Teddy Bear age 19
Owner/Photo: J. Lindley of
Morongo Valley, California

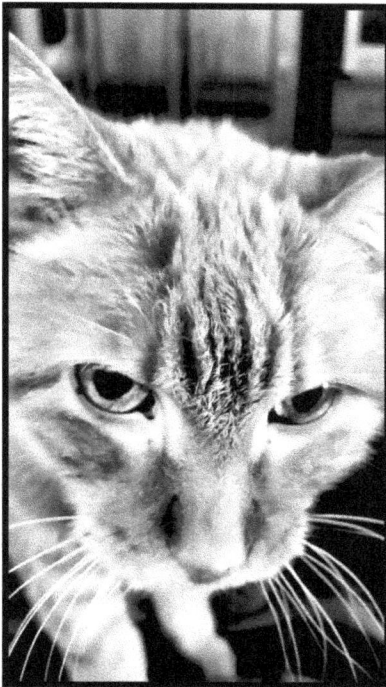

Cat: Sassy Cecilia age 26
Owner/Photo: Ginger Bingham of
Diamond, Missouri

Cat: Tisiphone age 10
Owner/Photo: Dorothy
Sheridan of Panama
City, Florida

Cat: Blue age 20
Owner/Photo: J. Lindley of
Morongo Valley, California

Cat: William age 11
Owner/Photo: Rems Turner of
Palm Springs, California

CHAPTER IV. BEHAVIOR CHANGES

NOBODY'S PERFECT, NOT EVEN ME.

BUT, I TRY VERY HARD, ESPECIALLY TO BE. - J. LINDLEY

The word behavior may be defined as the act of conducting oneself in a proper manner.[1] The cat, being a very sensitive animal, will often mirror her feelings, and emotions, in her behavior.[2] Your cat goes through a series of emotional changes throughout her entire life. Thus, her behavior is modified by the specific emotions she's feeling during the particular life stage (see chapter I Age). Also, influencing her emotions are hormones secreted into her body systems during the specific life stages. In other words, your cat's behavior may change drastically throughout her life. Your older cat will not necessarily appreciate the same things, or behave the same way, that she did as a kitten. During the lapse of years she has had plenty of time to sort things out.

A learned man once told me that the true key to this life is the number three. "Look around you," he said," and see with open eyes the threes." Funny, the more I've spent looking around the simpler things appear, in threes. He's right there is sufficient data to prove his theory of threes. For example, the immediate family unit of mother, father and child, or female, male and offspring. This applies to our entire reproductive basis. Next, applied to science and mathematics it is, once again, in threes, positive, negative and neutral. This principle also affects how we, as people, function in our own lives. In order to maintain a proper balance, and sanity, in our lives we must also have three phases. We must divide our time between rest, work and play. If any one of these things becomes too unbalanced our physical health and mental health will be threatened. What, you say, has this to do with the cat? The same actual principles of threes apply to our cats. They not only have three phases of life; growth, plateau and decline, their reproductive habits require a mate, of the opposite sex, and produce offspring, but, they also have three phases in behavior, normal, inappropriate, and unusual behavior. Even their daily behavior can be observed in three phases, rest, work and play. Our key to caring for our older cat, in reference to behavior is, again in threes, - love, patience and understanding.

1. NORMAL BEHAVIOR

What is normal for one may not necessarily be normal for another. According to Webster's New World Dictionary, normal is conforming with an accepted standard, or norm; natural; usual.[3] As applied to the cat it would mean what is natural or usual for that cat. Closer yet, your cat, would be what is considered as natural or usual to your individual cat. If you have two or more cats you will notice that what is normal for one will not necessarily be normal for all or even the same for any two. So, we must see normalcy in the cat on an individual basis. Also what was normal for your cat when it was younger may not be normal now. Many things natural, physical and emotional needs as well as nutritional and medical requirements change with age. Behavioral changes deal mostly with natural, physical and emotional needs. In a capsule, the older cat will most likely sleep more, be less tolerant of changes and seem more irritable or touchy.

SLEEPING

Possibly the biggest change you will notice in your older cat will be a change in sleeping habits. These changes will include the amount of time spent sleeping, or resting, the places chosen to nestle and, even more personal to your cat, changes in lying positions.

In prehistoric time miacids, the ancestor of modern day cats, were small animals. They spent time in trees, coming down, most likely at dusk and early dark, only to hunt smaller animals and for water, otherwise, catching what might be available in the trees.[4] Later on, the descended cats became much larger, with protective fangs and claws. They spent most of their time on the ground and had dens to sleep in. Being larger now, they didn't have to worry too much about being preyed upon, so they felt more secure and could sleep for longer periods. Their lives had developed into a regular pattern of sleeping, hunting and raising families. In the wild the cat is a refined killer. She does not go out and spend a lot of time hunting, as canines do, she sits and waits, stalks a little, runs, kills and eats. Then she has plenty of time to sleep until she requires another meal.[5] For the modern day feral cat, as well as the big cats, this pattern still exists.

The domestic house cat has the same basic sleep needs but the patterns are much different. The main reason for this is the human addition, YOU. You have given her security. Your cat does not fear, therefore she feels pretty comfortable in doing what she wants, when she wants to. One of the most complimentary things your cat can do is to openly sleep, curled up on your couch or in your favorite chair. She is actually telling you that she is comfortable and secure and, by being where your scent is, she is telling you that she loves you. Strange how sleeping can say so much.

Kittens spend about 80% of their young growing life sleeping. An adult cat, fully active and in good physical condition, spends about 60% of her life sleeping. Older adult cats may spend up to 80% of their time sleeping.[6] Cats do not sleep the same as humans, in periods of six to eight hours at a time. Cats sleep in shorter periods all through a twenty four hour period. The cat has two types of sleep, light sleep and deep sleep. Periods of light sleep may last from ten to thirty minutes. They are not quite fully relaxed and can wake up in an instant from light sleep. Deep sleep periods are shorter, maybe a maximum of ten minutes. During periods of deep sleep you may see your cat twitching, running, growling, lapping and even, sometimes, appearing to eat.[7] Although there is no real way of checking the contents of their dreams, obviously, they do dream. Sleeping patterns change with the life style of the cat. If you work part of the day and your cat is inside alone she may tend to sleep more during the day. Cats still have a tendency to be nocturnal. They still hunt at night. Even house cats enjoy lying close to a mouse-sound, hoping for a quick snack. My younger adult cats, those four to twelve years old, still prowl through the house at night checking the wall heater and cabinets. My older ones, those thirteen and up, seem to spend more time, both day and night, sleeping usually piled on my bed, or in front of the heater.

The next change you should notice, about your cat's sleeping, is where she chooses to rest. All cats seem to be sun-lovers, but the older ones are even more sun-loving. This is to be expected, because, as they age, their tolerance of the cold is decreased.[8] At night, my older ones first settle in front of the heater. If our heater happens to go out, Max, who's seventeen, will come upstairs, sit on my chest and sniffle in my face until I go and relight it. There have been a few nights when the heater area was so crowded that Max came up and crawled under the blankets with me. During the day, Max alternates between the sun-filled front room and my bed. Oftentimes, the older cats will prefer a soft bed to ease their thinning, bony bodies. Comforters make a lovely padded nest for them.

Cats actually make an art of sleeping. There is quite an array of sleeping positions, beginning with the most often seen curled position, extending full out to their entire length and flopped over on their back. It seems that the more comfortable, secure and warm they are, the more they open up. Most of the younger kittens, I've been able to observe, don't rest in such 'laid-out' positions, like the older ones. I'm sure it must be their high energy level. Unless kittens are completely exhausted, they will sleep on the lighter sleep level, more often, so they are able to get up and go immediately. The older cats, maybe having seen it all, or at least as much as they want to, are definitely more relaxed.

Minow (16) is certainly cozy under the covers. She spends her days and nights with her owner, Diane Petrucci of Sandwich, Mass.

Photo by J. Lindley

Max (17) prefers a sunny ledge.

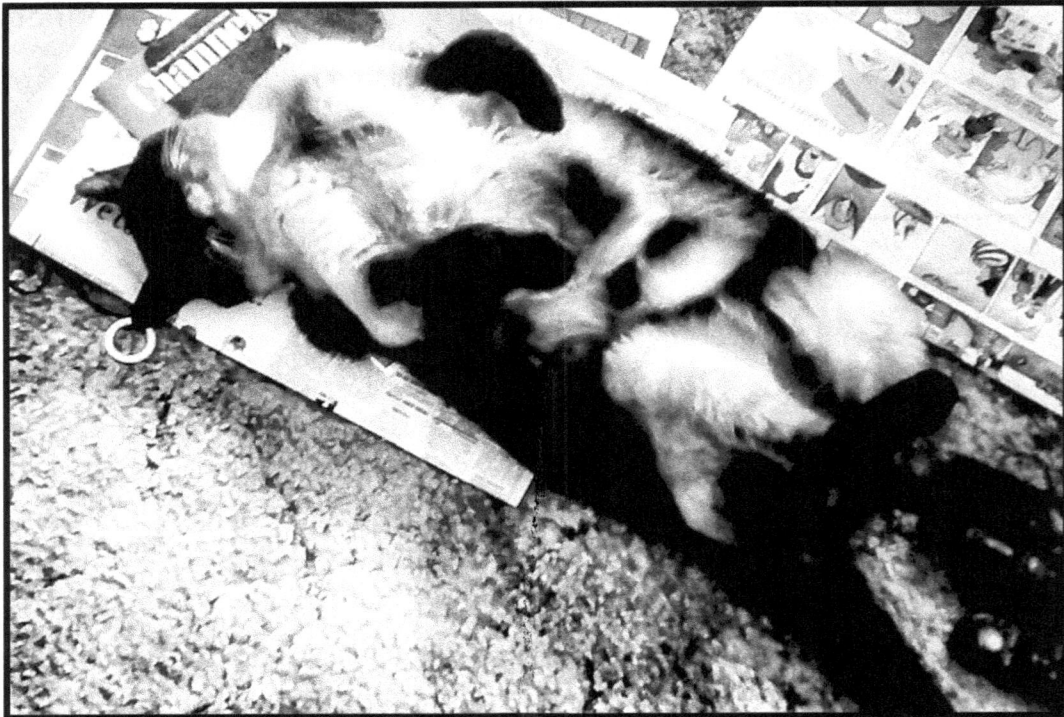

Shadow (19) lies fully open on her owner's current reading materials. She lives with Erica Newnham in Akron, Ohio.

WORK/PLAY

In the domestic house cat it's hard to define work separately from play. One begins as a mock form of the other, but also as training for the other. When the actual work, of hunting or family rearing is done, there's plenty of time for play. For the older cat the real work is pretty much done and now work and play merge as one.

For the younger cat, especially kittens, play is very important. Actual play begins while they are still with their mother. Gentle pawing at each other is the first sign of play. When the kittens are about five weeks old they go through, what I call, the jousting stage. They walk sideways at each other with backs arched and very fat tails. They look like little knights getting ready to joust. One pounces and the other goes straight up in the air. Then they chase each other around for a bit. Play, in kittens around 9 weeks of age, is a lot of pouncing, stalking and chasing, which is practice for future hunting. Play may occupy about 9% of the kitten's total time.[9] They do sleep a lot. The mother cat will be both playing and working with her kittens. If she is allowed out, we are talking about house cats, she may bring in live mice, or baby birds, let them go on your floor and call for her kittens to first, watch her attack and eat them, then later allow them to do the same. Much of the working time has been removed from the modern day house cat. Still, there are those periods at night, in the wee hours, when a particular gnawing sound will prick up their ears and they begin the chase for a quick mouse-snack. Watching my cats, I would say that this is both work and play for them. Another work/play time my older cats enjoy is morning bird-watching. My bedroom has a door that opens onto a small porch, on the second floor. The window in it allows full view of this porch area and roof edge rail. In Spring, birds make nests in the roof eaves. The nest making sound first attracts my older cats to the window. Once they are there, if the shade is down they enjoy the flitting bird shadows, if the shade is up they watch the real birds. The cats make a strange chattering, grinding sound, and appear to be almost drooling, as they watch the birds. Sometimes they get so involved that if a bird flies away, they will jump up and swat the window. It's a great game. I'm sure the results would be quite different if the window was open. It is still nice to see them get exercise and enjoy themselves.

Solitary play and what I call one-on-one play; when the cat either plays by herself or with her owner, as with objects rolled or string toys, also begins as kittens. Kittens love to bat at objects like small balls. Mine especially liked to chase after a ribbon. This play, particularly if an owner takes an interest, can last into the older years. Although my older cats spend a great amount of time sleeping, they still enjoy a good run after a shoelace or a jump in the air after a feather. I just have to remember to let them catch it once in awhile. They only really seem to slow down if arthritis sets in. Actually, a moderate amount of play is a good idea for an older cat, it keeps their muscles in tone and increases the blood circulation. In very old cats you may want to limit play. Watch them for signs of labored breathing or rapid tiring, these are signs of possible heart problems. You may need to limit play to a bare minimum and substitute grooming as your quality time together. While grooming, brushing, your cat, you can play simple hand-batting games. Grab-the-paw or stomach-touch are good. It is perfectly normal for the older cat to be less active but still want to enjoy your companionship. Play and love will keep your older cat 'young'-appearing and active for many years.

Jesse, at 18, doesn't get around much anymore, but he still enjoys a game of catch every morning, and any other time his owner, Kathy Hoffman in Kearney, NE, paused for the cause.

EMOTIONS

Your cat's emotions will change several times throughout her life. There may be several hormonal changes which influence her emotions but the most influential element is your cat's relationships with those around her and her environment. As a kitten, her first real relationship was with her mother. Her second relationship was with her siblings, which was concerned with competition for mother and all her attention. Mother is the center of her emotional feelings. This mother-relationship continues the entire life of your cat, with you substituted for her cat-mother. If you've acquired your cat young enough the feelings are more easily transferred from one to the other. You are now the center of her world and the object of her attention. The longer your cat has been with you, the stronger the love-bond will be. Even though your cat will have feline friends, her primary love will be for you.

Once your cat has reached her full physical growth, has been through her family raising, and been altered, she should begin to 'mellow-out' emotionally. Around four to eight years old the physical growth and the emotions seem to reach a plateau. This is a good time to take your cat to your veterinarian for a complete physical, as cats of this age seem to handle changes better.

As your cat begins the next age period of eight to ten years old, she may become more emotional. This is a very bad time to subject her to any drastic changes in her environment. Cats, of this age period, coming into my retirement home seem to grieve more for their lost owners. It takes them longer to make the adjustment to their change. Older cats have more problems adapting to new environments, anyway, but this age, between eight and ten seems to be the most difficult age period of all.

From twelve years on, you will be the most important entity in your cat's life. In multi-cat households, your cat may have a close friend or two but her sun will rise and set on you. When you are unhappy or upset, she will be there for you. She will nurse you through any illness just like a real Florence Nightingale. She will go out of her way to try to please you with extra attention. If your older cat has been brought up in a loving home she will enter her Golden Years gracefully. It is not so that all older cats become irritable with age. If your otherwise loving older cat does become grouchy there may be a psychological cause, as in relationships with others in her household, or a medical problem. In either event, she will need your help to become her old self again.

The most volatile times for an older cat seem to be the ages of eight to ten and twelve to fifteen. After fifteen years old your cat should become mellow again and begin to accept every day as it comes. My cats over fifteen years choose their friends from all age groups. Sometimes, my seventeen and eighteen year olds will seem to mother the younger ones and sit by anyone who isn't feeling quite up to snuff. On the other hand, there are a few of the oldest ones who like being fussed over and cleaned by the middle-aged ones. My middle-aged cats, those around eight to fifteen, seem to go both ways. Some like to take care of the oldest ones and some like to play with the youngest ones. The real key to normal behavior, no matter what age, is not what is normal for all cats in general but what is normal, or usual, for the one, your cat.

2. INAPPROPRIATE BEHAVIOR

There are many forms of abnormal, specifically inappropriate, behavior. Some of these, your cat will seem to think are perfectly normal but you may find them completely inappropriate. Where normal behavior becomes inappropriate depends on where you want to draw the line. Depending on the type of problem, you may need to take her to her veterinarian first to rule out a medical problem. Once medical problems are ruled out and your cat is physically all right the problem, most likely, will have a psychological, or emotional, cause. Each problem may have a different solution or they may have one major solution that links them together. Remember, each cat is an individual so what will work for one won't necessarily work for another.

LITTER BOX CHANGES

The problems of most serious concern seem to be changes in normal litter box habits, of urination or elimination. Your older cat will suddenly cease using her box and take her business to a more discrete location, ie. under chairs, dark corners, open closets or under your bed. She may also openly urinate on your kitchen counter, ugh! In the case of a multi-cat household, she may be trying to tell you that she needs another litter box, or the box needs to be cleaned more often. In the case of a single cat, the answer will be more complex. You first need to rule out any urinary or bowel problems. If urination, or defecation, is painful for her, she may associate the pain with her litter box, and stop using it. If it is a medical problem, as constipation which is very common in older cats, once the problem is treated, and cured, she should return to her normal litter box habits. Try to remember when the change first occurred. Did you change litter box cleaners, or the litter itself? I prefer to use clumping style litter in my house but I have several cats that won't use it. Although the coarser clay litter gets in their paws more, they prefer the clay to the finer grained clumping litters. Litter box placement may also be important to your older cat. If she is arthritic she may need an additional box closer to her sleeping quarters. A box with lower sides may help. As a last resort try a puppy pee pad or a newspaper in front of the box. Think about what caused the change first before getting too upset with her. A tirade, on your part will only upset her more. Please try to find a solution to her problem before considering giving her up. Many cats, coming into my retirement home, have been brought here because of bad litter box habits. I always feel that their owners could have tried a little harder for the happiness of the cat.

PERSONALITY CHANGES

The main problems of personality changes you may notice with your older cat will be aggressive behavior or the complete opposite, withdrawal. Older cats may have a tendency to be touchy or easily irritated. In a multi-cat household, both aggression and withdrawal can be a result of a squabble with another, in the household. With your attention this should work it self out, given a little time. Don't let your cat sulk, or hide, too long. Depression, in an older cat, can cause health problems. Withdrawal, in a single cat, is almost always a sign of medical problems. Aggression, in a single cat, is sometimes the sign of a brain tumor, and your veterinarian may be able to determine this. In the case of any abrupt change, your cat should be seen by a veterinarian. Simple hand biting during playing, or grooming, is not a form of true aggression. Hand biting is usually caused from excitement or it may even be intended as a love bite. Aggressive behavior directed, by your cat, toward a human, other than yourself, may be a result of jealousy. This type of jealous behavior can usually be remedied with more attention to your cat.

DESTRUCTIVE BEHAVIOR

Destructive behavior almost always has a psychological cause. It is usually an angry response to something that you have done, or your cat believes that you have caused to happen.[10] Jealousy, again, plays an important part in destructive behavior. Your cat may be jealous of your time spent, at work or with someone else. She may react in a number of different ways. Papers may be dragged around, chewed or urinated on. She may urinate on your bed or pillow. If you spend too much time sitting on your couch, she may urinate in that spot. She may destroy your favorite house plant or favored items of clothing. Specifically, eating of house plants, or wool and other foreign objects, has another side, a dietary problem (see diet chapter V), rather than jealousy. I've had jealous cats tear up my slippers and urinate in my shoes because they were unhappy with me. I never did find out why. I just made a point to give them a little extra attention and it never happened again. Whatever the problem, don't give up hope. I know destructive problems sometimes can be very heart breaking.

3. UNUSUAL BEHAVIOR

There are certain behavioral traits your older cat will display that are neither normal nor are they inappropriate. They fall into their own category, unusual. These traits may be of a very individualized nature, some are good, some just strange, others even disastrous for your cat.

Though often an inappropriate behavior, even toilet habits can have a good side. My sister moved into a house that came with its own cat, a neutered male named John. While she was moving furniture in, she was surprised to hear a tinkling sound coming from the bathroom. She looked at her boyfriend, across the table, and he looked back with equal surprise. Who else was in the house? What a shock, for her, to open the bathroom door to find a black kitty sitting on the toilet seat looking back. I don't remember ever hearing if John learned how to flush. She questioned John's former owner and apparently John's habit was self taught. Pretty smart kitty. I have one who raises his right paw when he wants something. I think he's picked it up from my dogs. Some of my cats have been snooze alarms. Almost exactly ten minutes after the alarm clock has gone off, they pounce on me or lick my nose until I get up. I call the good traits quirks and we usually enjoy them. Some unusual traits are all right for your cat while others are not, and they may need be seen by a veterinarian. These unusual behavior traits are: strange sleeping positions or places; unusual licking or washing; drooling and excessive salivation; 'fur-chewing'; anxiety and stress.

SLEEPING POSITIONS AND PLACES

The normal, most often seen, curled sleeping position affords your older cat some advantages. The curling takes up the least amount of space, protects her most vulnerable belly-side, and with the addition of the tail across her nose, reducing oxygen intake and promoting deeper sleep,[11] makes it an overall very comfortable position.

The curled position is a secure position. Your cat may take this secure curled position to even more 'secure' feeling places. Cats seem to love paper bags, cardboard boxes and older cats are definitely not an exception. Closet and cabinet shelves are also enjoyed, but can become dangerous if the door gets shut. One of my older cats found a drawer open and crawled in, making herself comfortable. My son, in his rush to dress for school, inadvertently closed the drawer. About midday I heard a faint meowing coming from the wall. She had been able to climb out the back of the drawer into the wall but was still unable to find a way out. I removed the drawer and a very happy cat rushed out.

Dawn (14 ½) surprises her mom, Patrice Sharkey, every time
She opens the closet. They share a home in Wautoma, WI.

Security is not always a dark closet. Sometimes it's demonstrated as sleeping curled with another cat, a stuffed toy, or the owner. Sometimes cats feel secure curled in a sink, until the faucet accidentally drips on them. I have several cats who like to sleep on clean laundry, if it's left out. On the other hand, there are older cats that prefer their owner's dirty laundry. Of course almost all cats like to sleep on warm dryers. The problem arises only if they sleep IN them. My cat, C.J., who's seventeen, likes to sleep on the arm of our couch with his legs hanging over. Some cats prefer high spots, like tops of book shelves or the refrigerator. These would be potentially dangerous, in the event of a fall, for an older cat. If your older cat prefers a specific high place, you should try to discourage her to do this by blocking the space, or at least putting pillows on the floor area to soften her accidental fall.

LICKING OR WASHING

Cats wash for many reasons: to smooth and clean their hair (to increase its efficiency as insulation); to calm themselves when they are uncomfortable, anxious or stressed; as a sign of affection to another, as well as to clean themselves. Cats also have that special ability to create vitamin D, by the action of sunlight, with saliva, on their groomed coat.[12] I used to tell people that cats wash themselves when they have nothing else to do because they spend so much time doing it. When an older cat washes, or licks, it may not only do itself, it may wash others around it as well. Some of my older cats seem to enjoy washing and cleaning, grooming, the younger ones. This mutual washing is often seen between two cats who particularly like each other, a form of affection. Licking and washing among themselves is considered very normal behavior.

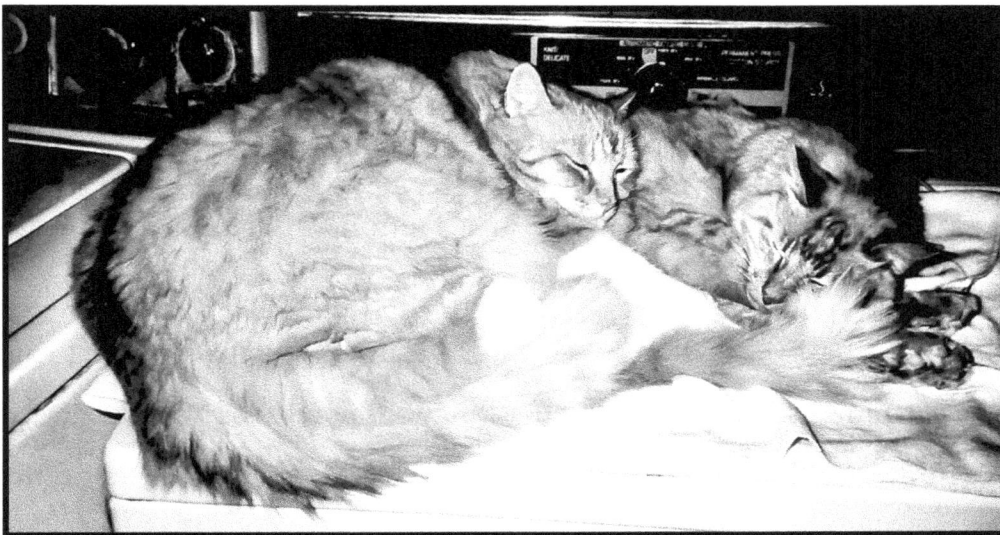

Tequila (18) and Leo (14) share their companionship and warmth on a dryer. They also share their lives with Kathleen Gibson and Elizabeth Nehf in Soquel, California.

Photo by J. Lindley

CJ (17) is almost always found relaxing on the arm of my couch,
unless of course he's sleeping on my bed.

Licking, or washing, becomes unusual when it is transferred to the human-owner. A gentle lick once in awhile is a common sign of affection. Some older cats feel so much sympathy for their people when they're crying, they will lick away the tears. This is also an understandable show of affection. Unusual aspects of licking are hair cleaning, i.e., the hair of your head, or worse, beard or armpit. I was awakened one night to my husband screaming, "Get her off me!" Our older cat, Princess, who usually sleeps with me, at night, had taken a fancy to his beard. Maybe it was some left over odor from dinner that bad attracted her. There she was licking contentedly away in his beard. It wasn't the licking that was bothering him, she was so happy she was kneading his chest with her claws. To tell the truth, I didn't know whether to laugh or grab and disturb Princess. I did notice a few days later that he decided to shave off his beard. In retrospect, I think Princess was first drawn by the food odor then became so engrossed in licking that it triggered memories of mom, and she began kneading in ecstasy.

Sometimes unusual licking can become dangerous. Point in case, K.C., an adult cat, craves certain kinds of plastic. At first it was bread wrappers. I thought she was after the remaining crumbs. More than often it's a store plastic with no food on it. Fortunately her desire is purely a fetish and she hasn't tried to eat the plastic bags yet. I have to admit I've had daymares of her choking on the plastic. Lately her strange plastic desires have begun to wane. Unusual licking, or washing, doesn't happen too often. If it becomes stranger it might be worth looking into possible nutritional deficiencies.

DROOLING AND EXCESSIVE SALIVATION

Drooling can be compared, somewhat, to unusual licking. It can be a result of a linked emotion, such as a memory of mom.[13] As the kitten nurses it drools and salivates. Your older cat may be over stimulated by some sort of emotion and the salivary glands are triggered.

There are several medical possibilities to explain drooling. The most common oral problem in an older cat is gingivitis (see Chapter II Mouth, the Oral Cavity). Signs of severe gingivitis include drooling, clinically known as ptyalism. Associated with this type of drooling are bad breath (halitosis) and difficulty in chewing, or eating.[14] Another possibility would be a salivary mucocele, or cyst, which forms when a salivary duct is injured, causing saliva to collect in the tissues and develop a saclike cyst.[15] If the cyst were to open, excessive drooling would definitely result. Stomach upsets will also cause drooling. It is more normal for older cats to develop dry mouth, but, there are always reverse symptoms. It's always best to have anything that's really excessive checked, by your veterinarian, to rule out medical problems.

'FUR-CHEWING'[16]

I have two older cats, and one young adult (age 6 yrs.) that display this peculiar form of behavior. The oldest one, Elvira, seventeen years, is in incredible health with the exceptions of one folded ear and a fairly bald stripe down the middle of her back. When Elvira came, about three years ago, I thought this was a reaction to her stress, from relocation. I suspect, since the stripe continues most of the year, that it may be an allergic reaction, or even a hormonal imbalance. Cortocosteroids might clear her up but also might upset her, otherwise, good health. Since she is seventeen it's best to just leave it alone, unless it begins to bother her. The other cat, Gucci, is a short haired black cat and about twelve years of age. She licks the hair off her belly area when she feels stressed. Belly hair and back hair are slow to grow so it always looks worse than it is.

First, rule out any medical problems. There are organic diseases that might trigger the hair chewing response. As far as a behavioral pattern, psychological stress-related hair loss and skin inflammation are uncommon disorders in the cat.[17] Psychogenic alopecia is characterized by single, or multiple, areas of hair loss, especially a "stripe" down the back, or even in a symmetrical pattern, mimicking an endocrine disorder.[18] The clue is that the underlying skin will be normal. When my cat, Kona, a ten year old, first came, she developed a stress-stripe. As the hair grew back, it grew in a slightly darker color. Kona is a mixed Siamese with variegated brown colors, so this extra color looked nice, anyway. When hair grows in on the belly side I've not noticed any color variation.

ANXIETY AND STRESS

Anxiety and stress are the worst type of behaviors your cat can display and, sometimes, they can be the hardest to diagnose. Anxiety is more of an external display of various expressions, while stress is more an internal turmoil, both of which may include physical problems.[19] Either one can be extremely harmful for the older cat.

Anxiety may be defined as the mental distress brought on by apprehension of danger, usually associated with fears or worries.[20] Some anxiety is discharged quickly by the cat, as in sudden aggressive behavior or biting. An anxious cat may be an attacker, taking out her feelings on those closest to her, which might be you or a companion cat. A good example of this was my cat, Stokley. When I had my first two cats, I felt it was cruel to keep them inside all the time. So, I allowed them out during the day, specifically on weekends, when I was home from work. One Saturday, I heard the screech of car tires. I held my breath and quickly prayed as I ran out. Stokley had gone across the street and, on his return home, hadn't run fast enough and was bumped. He ran into the bushes at the side of my house. When I went to reach in after him, he bit me. He also hissed and growled when I looked in at him, strange behavior for my otherwise calm, affectionate cat. It took me about ten minutes of coaxing before I could get him calm enough to reach in so I could move him out and check him over. This type of response was severe anxiety induced by extreme trauma.

Anxiety can be caused by a number of things, but only those which are particularly upsetting, or exciting, to your cat. Your cat can become anxious while you're grooming her. She enjoys the petting and grooming so much that she becomes excited, gets an energy charge and releases it in the form of a bite. The feeling of good becomes so great that she becomes anxious.

Another, less common, form of anxiety display is excessive washing. Your older cat may associate washing with the licking and cleaning by her mother. When she is feeling upset, or insecure, she may resort to washing herself in order to calm down. Sometimes older cats when anxious will wash all the hair off their bellies or even their lower back. As in Stokley's accident, anxiety is the result of, or the cat's response to, a situation. It is usually short term, may last a few days or weeks at the most, then your cat should return to normal.

Stress is usually a much longer term situation. It, too, is a result of, or a response to, a change. Comparatively, anxiety is usually associated with a sudden change and a quick reaction - stress is a more subtle reaction to a specific change. Stress is held internally and, if not alleviated, can build and build until your cat becomes very ill. Stress can cause symptoms of simple weepy eyes to upper respiratory problems, as well as trigger asthma attacks. It can also trigger bouts of cystitis or constipation. Your older cat is vulnerable to stress because of her physical aging. When she feels stressed, the weakest part of her body, her stress-target, will be attacked. Stress can also affect the skin and coat, which becomes patchy and dry. Stress may also be an underlying cause of inappropriate behaviors, i.e. house-soiling, aggression, withdrawal and destructive behaviors. If it is caused by another cat it may cause her to gulp her food which will lead to vomiting, drooling or excessive washing. The most serious effect I've seen with stress is depression. Sometimes cats, particularly those who go through a traumatic emotional change, as in abandonment, get severely depressed. They become listless, withdrawn, despondent, and refuse to eat. Refusal to eat brings on its own problems (see Chapter V Dietary Problems). Sometimes a vitamin B shot will help. If the depressed older cat, such as one who misses her owner, can not be turned around, she may will herself to death. Cats are very strong willed and when you combine this with the strongest of emotions, love, you can have big problems. The only real antidote is love, but if the cat isn't receptive, I know of nothing that will work. It can be very heart breaking.

SUMMING IT UP

The meaning of behavior is to conduct oneself in a proper manner.[21] Who's really to say what's proper? The cat is very much an individual and her set of rules for behavior will not always coincide with ours. If there is a great conflict of views it's time to make a change. Older cats don't often accept changes easily so you need to have patience.

Normal behavior patterns, of work, play and sleep, for the cat, can sometimes interfere with our life styles. For example, if you work during the day, your cat may be bored without you and sleep most of the day. When night comes and you want to sleep, guess what happens? Playtime! Lovely things as romp across the bed, knocking things around in the kitchen or running up and down the hall, begin to happen. How do you stop this? You need something to occupy your cat during the day. You could leave a radio, or TV, on for company, or you might even consider getting another cat.

If you cannot change your cat's particular behavior, perhaps you can make some adjustments so it becomes acceptable to both of you. My late husband used to say, "Turn a negative into a positive, but if you can't do that, at least try to meet somewhere in the middle". Better, yet, make a learning experience out of it. Most, if not all, cat magazines have a column written by a behavioral psychologist, to whom you can direct questions.

According to a recent article in I Love Cats, between fifty to seventy percent of cats taken to shelters are there because of behavioral problems.[22] The numbers of cats euthanized at impound shelters are staggering. It is said that for every problem there is a solution, sometimes it's just a challenge to find it. But, please don't let your kitty become another shelter statistic.

In a multitude of ways, my learned friend's theory of threes is correct, but with one more number. That number is one. The main one influencing factor in your cat's life is YOU. You can make the difference. Don't give up on your old baby because she seems grouchy or unreachable, as we all have bad days. Hold her, love her and soon she'll be her sweet purring self again.

NOTES

1 *Webster's New World Dictionary, (N.Y.: Warner Books, 1990): 55 Warner Books Paperback Ed.*

2 *Carol C. Wilbourn, Cat Talk, What Your Cat Is Trying To Tell You, (N.Y.: MacMillan Pub. Co., 1979): 15.*

3 *Webster's New World Dictionary, Warner Books Paperback Ed. (N.Y.: Warner Books, 1990): 401.*

4 *Dennis Kelsey-Wood, The Age of Mammals, The Atlas of Cats of the World, (Neptune, N.J.: TFH, 1989): 51.*

5 *Desmond Morris, Catwatching (N.Y.: Crown Pub. 1986): 128-129.*

6 *Cat Naps, Understanding Cats, Reader's Digest Illustrated Book of Cats (N.Y.: Reader's Digest 1992): 225.*

7 *ibid.*

8 *June Kirvan-Tuttle, Jeffrey E. Barlough, Mordecai Siegal and Leo A. Wuori, Aging Cats and Disorders, The Cornell Book of Cats (N.Y.: Villard Books div of Random House, 1992): 309.*

9 *Katherine A Houpt, Feline Behavior The Cornell Book of Cats (N.Y.: Villard Books div of Random House, 1992): 58.*

10 *Personal observations - J. Lindley.*

11 *Wendy Christensen, "The Cat's Revealing Tail", Cat Fancy Magazine (March 1995): 11*

12 *Desmond Morris, Catwatching (N.Y.: Crown Pub. 1986): 35-36.*

13 *Carol C. Wilbourn, Cat Talk, What Your Cat Is Trying To Tell You (N.Y.: MacMillan Pub, 1979): 30.*

14 *Jeffrey E. Barlough, Linda Susan Jorgensen and Ronald C. Riis, Sensory Organs and Disorders, The Cornell Book of Cats, (N.Y.: Villard Books div of Random House, 1992): 163.*

15 *Roy V.H. Pollock, Digestive System and Disorders, The Cornell Book of Cats (N.Y.: Villard Books div of Random House, 1992): 227.*

16 *"Fur-Chewing" - Although this is the recognized name, fur is usually applied to fur-bearing animals, those used for pelts. Therefore, hair is probably more professionally accepted.*

17 *Danry W. Scott, Skin and Disorders, The Cornell Book of Cats (N.Y.: Villard Books div of Random House, 1992):157.*

18 *ibid, pg 158.*

19 *Carol C. Wilbourn, Cat Talk, What Your Cat Is Trying To Tell You (N.Y.: MacMillan Pub, 1979): 46 & 53.*

20 *ibid, pg 46.*

21 *Webster's New World Dictionary, Warner Paperback Ed. (N.Y.: Warner Books, 1990): 55.*

22 *Cora Weatherford, "Breaking Bad Cat Behavior", I Love Cats, (March/April 1996): 62.*

CHAPTER V. WHAT YOU CAN DO

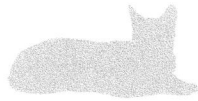

T his is probably the most important chapter in this book. Once you have read all about the normal expected aging changes you should have enough knowledge to be able to put the information into practice during your cat's every day life. This chapter will give you the guidelines to do this. Please remember, these are only guidelines, not the final word. Each cat is an individual, so each subject may need to be adjusted to suit your particular cat. As in Chapter IV much of this text is based upon my own observations. Running a shelter for cats has given me much information to choose from. In total I've been able to share the lives of 1500 cats and each one has had something to offer.

In most cases, the care you've given your cat in the past will reflect in the care you give your cat now, as well as what she'll need in the future. If she was healthy during her growing period, and kept current on all required vaccinations, chances are really good she will remain healthy throughout her life. Diet is of great importance, for without a proper diet, suited to her physical needs, she will not retain her good health.

Once health and proper diet are maintained the next influencing factor is her comfort. If she is comfortable in her surroundings then she will be at ease and peaceful. In this way cats are like people, once they are at peace with themselves and their surroundings, they can handle little changes relatively well. It is not yet known, clinically, what causes diabetes or hyper-thyroidism, the two most common ailments of older cats, nor is it known why only some cats are prone to arthritis and cancer, while others are not. Things like this we must deal with as they come along. As long as your cat knows she's loved she'll trust you to see that she's properly cared for during her time of need. We can never be fully prepared for when the final time will come but we can make the time we have to share the best possible.

IN HOME CARE

Perhaps the easiest things we can do, for our older cat, are those things we do, unthinkingly, on a normal basis. The first loving pat in the morning, as we tumble out of bed and head for the kitchen, starts their day off great. If you work, leave a radio on for company during the day. It's not you, but it will keep her from feeling too lonely. If you're home, she'll have her security and love. Even if you're busy, take a few minutes just to see what she's doing and maybe give her an extra pet. My old house cats seem to enjoy just lying around during the day. Their favorite time seems to be in the evenings. If supper smells especially nice they will cluster about the floor hoping for a handout. I spend my last few hours relaxing in front of the television, with one or two, sometimes more, alternating places on my lap. Evenings are usually the best time for grooming and rubbing, as we're all more relaxed and have more time to spend together. Seems like the older they get the closer they want to be. Please, give in to your cat when she seeks your affection. It is an easy time to check her for any problems and exchange your mutual feelings of love.

1. HOME EXAM

There are many things you can check on a daily basis, just by simple observations, but there are some you should check on as a regular routine. The older your cat becomes, the more often your routine examination should become. You may wish to refer to the chart, following Chapter II, for normal expectations. Anything you find abnormal you should check with your veterinarian, by phone first, to see how important it might be. Remember the older your cat, the more difficult it is for her when she is ill.

In order to begin your home exam you must first consider what is normal, for your cat, and what is expected during particular times of the year. For example, it is normal for my cats, with allergies, to have an occasional weepy eye or to be sneezing especially when the weather changes, or the wind blows. So, using the information in the preceding chapter should be able to determine what would be considered normal for your cat. Using information available to me,[1] I have put together the following check list. You may either use it, or you may wish to adapt it to your own cat's needs.

GENERAL ALL-PURPOSE EXAM

1. Eyes - should be clear and bright. Also acceptable would be a mild clear weeping, depending on age and weather; and a slight opaque appearance due to lens aging. Problems: abnormal discharge or uneven pupils, red, yellow or inflamed sclera and the appearance of the third eyelid. Gently lift the lids to check.

2. Ears - Should be clean, no dirty sludge or draining; Problems: head shaking, rubbing or scratching.

3. Nose - A slight, damp, moisture, possible, a slight clear runny nose (with extreme age) or occasional sneezing. Problems: excessive, mucus discharge.

4. Mouth - Gums should be pink, with clean teeth. In extreme age watch for gingivitis (red lined gums) and tartar buildup. Problems: Your cat will show sensitivity by difficult chewing, often dropping her food, excessive drooling or salivation, or

141

pawing at her mouth, or side of her face or chewing on one side. Remember, bad gums can lead to loose or broken teeth.

5. Coat - clear skin, shiny and silky coat. Problems: dull or greasy coat and flaky skin. Unkempt patchy coat is usually a problem sign. Bumps may be allergies, but lumps may be tumors.

6. Breathing - should be normal and regular. Problems: unusual panting or gasping and choking.

7. Eating - Her appetite should be regular. Some cats are served twice a day while others prefer to have dry food available all the time. Problems: Lack, or loss, of appetite is usually the first indication that something is wrong.

8. Body - Normal adult weight is 8-12 pounds. You may need to alter this according to your breed, and age, of cat. Actual rib bones should not be visible, even in extreme age. Although obesity can be a problem, a slightly overweight cat may be all right.

9. Behavior - What ever is normal for your cat shouldn't change too drastically with age; may be more emotionally sensitive. Problems: Unusual aggressiveness or withdrawal. Hiding is often an indication of illness.

10. Toilet Habits - Normal litter box habits shouldn't change with age, unless your cat is arthritic. Water consumption and urination should balance out. Problems: Inappropriate urination or straining may be indications of urinary problems.

11. Any unusual odors present - foul breath, or odor about the head area, may signal infections, sweet breath may indicate urinary or kidney problems (i.e. diabetes mellitus).

12. Activity - It is considered to be perfectly normal for the older cat to slow down a little and sleep more. Problems: listlessness, lethargy, unusual limping or refusal to move.

13. Vomiting - during hairball season it would be expected, to remove ingested hair. Some older cats, especially those in multi-cat households, gulp air as they eat, in which case they may vomit shortly after eating. Problems: frequent vomiting.

14. Diarrhea or constipation - Either could be normal for your aging cat, depending on her system, although constipation may be more common. Problems: unusual straining or blood-tinged stools.

15. Watch closely for signs of hyperthyroidism as it is quite common in cats over 10 years old. Typical signs include: rapid weight loss, but ravenous appetite, restlessness and hyperactivity, increased thirst and urination and strong, rapid heart beat.

Anything that is abnormal, or unusual, should be checked by your veterinarian. Problems, if caught soon enough, can be either eliminated or controlled, before the overall health of your cat suffers.

NOTE

[1] *Owner's Guide to Giving A Home Health Exam, Perspectives On Cats, a newsletter from the Cornell Feline Health Center, (Winter 1991): 1.*

2. GROOMING, PETTING AND BODY MASSAGE

Grooming depends on what type of hair your cat has. If she has a long, fluffy, Persian-type coat chances are good that you'll be brushing her more often than if she's a shorter haired lady. There are many grooming aids available, all styles (and teeth) of brushes and combs to the cats' self- groomers, i.e. the corner Cat-A-Comb.™ For my longhairs I prefer the slicker-style brushes, and for the shorthairs a softer brush. I also like the brushes that combine the wire on one side with the soft bristles on the other For those of you who may be new at grooming, there is a fantastic idea out called grooming gloves. They are covered with a special nub-like texture that removes the loose and shedding hair as you stroke your cat. Whatever you use, grooming is important to reduce the amount of hair your cat might otherwise ingest. Grooming is not limited to just brushing. Regular grooming should include checking your cat's eyes and ears and clipping long claws. It is also a good time to check her for any unusual odors. Your grooming technique, and the amount of time spent doing it, may depend on how much your cat will tolerate. I find that my older cats do not tolerate baths too well, so I often use a damp towel for cleaning purposes. Older cats may have sensitive skin so they may want to limit your time. As you brush your cat, keep in mind your own hair, brush in short strokes and take it easy on mats or tangles. Persistence and patience are the keys to good enjoyable grooming sessions.

Did you know there is a proper way to pet your cat? According to Lori Dillman,[1] in an article How To Pet a Cat, there are six different techniques: the dribble, the stroke, the ear and chin scratch, the tail squeeze, the tummy rub and the paw spread. The dribble refers to the most common pat, as comparing it to the dribbling of a basketball. A true cat lover would vary between the stroke and the ear and chin scratch. The tummy rub, tail squeeze and paw spread would normally be a more personal thing between you and your cat. When I first encounter a cat, not my own, I usually approach it with my hand held palm side up and flat. This is so the cat can first smell me to know I will do her no harm. Next, I slightly cup my hand and scratch her ears. I've learned, the hard way, not to approach a cat with over turned hand from above, i.e. on the head, it seems to be a dominance sign and they don't always appreciate it. If the cat enjoys the scratching, I usually move to both ears then massage their neck. Unless I continue to give a complete massage, I will end a petting session by moving my cupped hand over the cat's back and gently pulling her tail. Someone once told me that this gentle tail pulling helps to align the back bones. Once again, the petting techniques will vary with the cat's tolerance.

One thing my older cats tolerate very well is a whole body massage. As a matter of fact I also appreciate a good massage. The benefits of giving your cat a massage are practically endless. It will relax their aging muscles, help to limber their stiff joints, relieve arthritis pain, help improve circulation besides giving them the comfort of your loving touch, and reinforcing the emotional bond between you. Massage is a little more than rubbing the sore or stiff spots. It takes a bit of work, but you should be pleased with the results. Again, as in grooming and petting, techniques will vary according to what your cat will tolerate, and how much your fingers are willing to work. I normally begin at the head and work towards the rear, then down the hind legs and finally the front legs and paws. If your cat has allergies, or sinus problems, you may want to concentrate more on her face, around her eyes. If she has arthritis, you should pay more attention to the shoulders, back and hip areas. I begin all my massage sessions by first relaxing myself. I shake out my arms, wrists, and flex my fingers. Then, I try to position my cat so it is most comfortable and fairly relaxed. I find that speaking to her before and during the massage helps her to relax more. I begin touching, as in petting, a cupped hand to rub the ear. After the ears, I move to the neck, rubbing, with my hand still cupped, in a circular motion. If I'm massaging Max, who has sinus problems, I then move to his face. Using my thumbs, while cupping his head in my hands, I massage around his eyes. After his face I move on to his back. I hold my hand in a bent position, so that it covers both sides of his spine. Then, I rub in a circular motion down his back to his hips. I then massage one hind leg after the other, including both paws and move on to the front legs. Sometimes Max wishes his stomach rubbed, as well, in which case he'll roll over and allow me to gently rub his stomach. Once done, Max, usually, gets up and arches his back. I give him a quick stroke down his back bone and end with a gentle tail pull. It always makes me feel good to see how much Max enjoys the massage. A few final tips, on massaging; don't use oil, just your warm hands, stroke in the direction of the hair, and, evenings are usually the best time. One word of caution, don't massage a cat with a sprain or that has a serious viral disease, it may make situations worse.

Now, go ahead and enjoy, I know your cat will.

NOTE

[1] *Lori Dillman, "How To Pet A Cat", I Love Cats magazine, (Mar/Apr 1996): 18*

3. DIET

The diet you choose, for your cat, will depend, mostly, on what is available to you. The type of cat food available varies in different parts of the country and all over the world. In the United States we are offered a variety of prepared cat food, both packaged and canned. Reputable cat food manufacturers, in our country, have had enough experience, through mandated feeding trials, to produce cat foods with the required proper ingredients, although the amounts may vary with each manufacturer. In other countries, people must rely on key foods as a source for proper nutrition. If the food you provide is not adequate severe nutritional problems can develop.

The cat has a relatively short digestive tract[1] so, for quick absorption, she needs foods that are highly digestible, as well as those that supply the right nutrients. Being a true carnivore (meat eater) her metabolism is suited to a diet high in protein and fat. Basically, cats need vitamins, minerals, fatty acids, a good source of protein, taurine and, of course water. Dietary concerns for the older cat are, first, the amounts of protein, fat, carbohydrates and, then essential vitamins and minerals. There is an old saying "you are what you eat". If your cat is what she eats she would be part chicken, fish and cow, with a little mouse, not to exclude food colorings and preservatives. She would be quite an unusual looking animal. Cats, like humans, will not always eat what's good for them. But, since an adult cat can eat up to 20 times her own weight in a year[2] we need to make sure that what she does eat is at least healthy for her.

Butterball (17) lives with Les and Alice Caldwell, in Twentynine Palms, Calif.

Collage Art by J. Lindley

CONTENTS AND SOURCES

The amount of protein, you feed your cat, is the number one concern. Protein is a complex combination of amino acids, the organic building blocks of life. The quality of protein is determined by the proper balance of the amino acids. Some of these amino acids are nonessential, they are manufactured by the cat, some are essential, must be provided for her. A prime example of an essential amino acid is taurine. When the cat's diet does not contain adequate amounts of taurine, a heart problem, dilated cardiomyopathy, may develop. Protein is necessary for growth and repair of soft body tissues and strong bones, as well as an energy source. Recommended amounts for your adult cat will vary according to her life style. The average healthy adult cat's diet should contain 30-45 percent protein.[3] Adult maintenance diets contain 30% protein.[4] My older cats, since they are somewhat under stress, do better on at least 34% to 38% protein. These percentages are figured on a dry matter basis. The amounts of available protein in canned foods vary from 8% to 12% (some even higher) depending on the manufacturer.[5] If your provided diet is too low in protein your cat may over eat to try to make up the difference. Food sources for protein include meat, fish, poultry, eggs and cheese. Soybean meal, a plant source, is an excellent source of protein, and is used by many commercial cat food manufacturers.

Fats are a concentrated source of energy. Fats can provide 2 1/4 times more energy than protein.[6] Dietary fats are made up of fatty acids, both essential and nonessential. Fats are necessary to maintain a good healthy, shiny coat and soft skin. They also act as a carrier for fat soluble vitamins, ie. A, D and E, and give taste to the food. The recommended amount of dietary fat for the healthy adult cat is a minimum of 10%, and not more than 30%.[7] Sources are animal and vegetable oils and fats.

Carbohydrates are made up of sugars and starches.[8] They are used to provide the cat a quick form of energy. Although they may make up to 40% of commercial dry foods, they are not an absolute necessity for the older cat.[9] Excess carbohydrates are stored by the cat's body as extra weight and may contribute to obesity. Some older cats may have intolerance to a carbohydrate known as lactose, a milk sugar.[10] There are certain carbohydrates, dietary fiber that your older cat can benefit from. Fiber is a term used for plant parts, i.e. stems, leaves, seeds or pulp, and is sometimes referred to as roughage or bulk.[11] Fiber absorbs water, lends bulk to the intestinal contents, stimulates movement of the intestinal tract and increases the bulkiness of the stool. This combined action, of fiber, may aid in constipation problems, common to older cats. Food sources rich in carbohydrates are potatoes, cereals and bread.

Vitamins are also a nutritional requirement. Vitamins are organic compounds required for normal life functions, including growth, development and reproduction. As applied to the older cat, they maintain a balance between constructive and destructive cell changes and help resist disease.[12] Several vitamins are unstable and may be destroyed by light, heat, oxidation, moisture or fat rancidity. So, sufficient amounts are required in the diet to maintain minimum daily vitamin requirements. In a normal balanced diet it is not necessary for you to supplement these vitamins. Vitamin (and mineral) supplementation should only be done as recommended by your veterinarian. In the case of extremely old or old cats under stress, supplementation may be given to encourage appetite, particularly if the cat has been ill.

Ash is also contained in all nutritionally complete and balanced diets. I was always taught to stay away from foods high in ash content because it was associated with urinary problems. This has proven to be untrue.[13] Ash is a term used to describe the residue, of mineral content, remaining after a food sample is burned for 2 hours at 600 degrees centigrade. It is composed of essential minerals, i.e. calcium, phosphorus, potassium, sodium chloride and magnesium.[14] Therefore, if you feed a diet too low in ash, mineral deficiencies can develop. Minerals are necessary to help maintain the body's acid-base (electrolyte) balance, tissue structure and fluid balance. They also serve as components of enzymes and organic compounds necessary to the cat's body.[15]

Water, although not usually considered as a food nutrient, is most important to the diet. All animals need water to exist. Water plays an important role in all functions of the animal's body, i.e. digestion, excretion and circulation. It carries nutrients, builds tissues and maintains temperature. It aids in cushioning joints and internal organs and lubricates body tissues. It also helps salts and electrolytes circulate through the body. Because cats are able to concentrate their urine, conserving some of their water, they can handle dehydration (water loss) much better than dogs or humans.[16] Older cats, however, are very susceptible to dehydration. Water loss can be attributed to diarrhea, vomiting and excessive urination. Water intake should be carefully watched, especially if you feed dry cat food. During periods of unusual stress, or weather changes, your cat may drink more water. Fresh water should be available for her at all times.

UNUSUAL DIETS

Feeding your cat a diet of something other than one that is commercially prepared can be very tricky. There is really no way to know if your cat is getting adequate amounts, other than health problems as they arise. Even though the cat is a true carnivore, a diet of all raw meat can be harmful. For one thing, raw meat tends to spoil quickly. A diet of primarily organ meat, i.e. heart or liver, would be too low in calcium and other necessary vitamins and minerals. Even though your cat is no longer growing she still needs calcium for strong bones. Remember, the original carnivores not only ate the meat of their prey but chewed on the bones as well, while ingesting the nutrients from grains that the prey had eaten. A diet of all raw fish, even though might be favored by your cat could result in a thiamine (B1) deficiency. People who are devout vegetarians may wish to feed their cats on a strict vegetarian diet. This is not wise as cats require certain essential amino acids, i.e. taurine, and certain vitamins, i.e. vitamin A and niacin, present only in meat sources. Soy, even though a good protein source, would not be an adequate diet. Your cat still needs some meat, and even the occasional mouse would not be quite enough. In countries where commercially manufactured foods are unavailable, a diet for an older cat would need to include: plenty of high quality protein food, i.e. fish, meat and poultry; a variety of vegetables and fruit; a little lard (animal fat) and vegetable oil, occasionally for hairballs and constipation.

Recently there has been a trend to feeding raw meat to both cats and dogs. Cats, being carnivores, require the meat, but they need grain and the by products. By products are usually innards that the cat would have gotten from their prey. The grains help with fiber intake and will help keep feces more solid, as opposed to a raw meat diet.

SPECIAL DIETS

Special diets are those suited to your cat's medical or physical needs. There are quite a few of them to choose from, but it's best to consult your veterinarian before putting your cat on any special diet. Medically, older cats are prone to kidney disease, or renal failure, urinary tract problems, constipation and heart problems. Although, all these problems are associated with old age your cat may, or may not, have them. If she does display a problem your veterinarian will most likely prescribe one suited to her condition.

The other types of special diets are geared for the physical activity of your cat. Older cats may be prone to weight gain if they are less active, particularly if fed a diet too rich in carbohydrates and fat. Be careful in choosing a diet, because your older cat still needs good quality protein. Read the labels carefully. Adult maintenance diets usually begin with 30% protein. Older cats, and cats under stress, will probably require a minimum of 34% protein.[17] Diets for over weight cats come in names such as Inside, Less Active or Reduced Activity. Please remember that a cat who is big and robust at fourteen years may not be so at sixteen as cats most commonly get thinner with age. A special diet too soon could be harmful to her.

DIETARY ABNORMALITIES
OBESITY

Obesity is the most common diet-induced disease in cats.[18] It has been determined that if your cat is 15% over her normal weight she is considered to be obese.[19] The amount of fat stored by the body, usually from crude fat and carbohydrates, increases over time. If your older cat is not active enough she will not be able to burn off the additional body fat and she may become obese. However, just because she may look a bit over weight doesn't mean that she's obese. A good way to tell her weight is to feel her ribs. Unless she's extremely old and thinning, you should not be able to see her ribs. At normal weight you should be able to feel all her ribs. If she's obese you may not be able to feel any of them. Another way to tell is by her normal activity. Obese cats, when walking often sway from side to side.[20] They seem slower and very lazy. They will have difficulty jumping up on things, ie. their favorite chair or couch.[21] If your cat is big but still very active, she would be considered overweight but not necessarily obese. True obese cats are usually observed at middle-ages, i.e. four through ten years.[22] It is more normal for an older cat to be thin. However, I have seen several obese cats at twelve years old.

Obesity can be very unhealthful for the older cat. The extra weight not only can be stressful for her joints but it can aggravate arthritis. Shortness of breath can bring on respiratory problems and cause stress on her heart, shortening her life span. Should she require surgery, obesity would be a health risk.[23] There is also a greater risk, 2.2-fold, that your cat could develop diabetes mellitus.[24] If you feel your cat is obese you should have her seen by your veterinarian. Obesity can be controlled by a calorie reduced diet. You should always consult your veterinarian before placing her on any diet. You may need to gradually mix the new diet in her normal food so her system becomes used to the new taste. If your cat does not accept her new diet, she may refuse to eat. If she refuses to eat more than two meals it might be wise to put her back on her old diet. Should an obese cat go without eating too long she may develop hepatic lipidosis. Hepatic lipidosis is described as a system shock, in this case deprivation of food, which causes the liver to malfunction. The cat becomes jaundiced and her liver becomes enlarged, with an accumulation of fat. It is thought that this is brought on by the immediate drastic reduction of proteins needed for liver function.[25] To help a cat with hepatic lipidosis, vitamin supplements are necessary to stimulate appetite so she will begin eating again. Veterinary assistance is mandatory as the survival rate may be only 65% of cats with severe symptoms.[26] Unfortunately, I've had some first hand experience with hepatic lipidosis. Some cats, coming to me, don't want to eat right away, as they are often stressed. I keep a tube of vitamin supplement on hand at all times. I've not noticed hepatic lipidosis in the normal weight cats, just the overweight ones. I've been extremely fortunate to have been able to pull most of them through their time of stress-related starvation, but I have lost a few to hepatic lipidosis. I have learned to pay close attention to the eating habits of all my new cats.

ANOREXIA

Anorexia, or progressive weight loss, can be a serious problem in older cats. It is normal for an old cat to be thin but not too thin. Too this is a signal that your cat may have kidney disease, a tumor, diabetes mellitus, liver disease or other serious conditions.[27] Anorexic cats seem to be unusually weak.[28] They tend to stagger.[29] They sniff at their food, and then walk away.[30] If your cat displays this problem you need to take her to the veterinarian for a complete check up.

WOOL CHEWING, HOUSEPLANT EATING AND PICA

Wool chewing, not always a problem specific to just older cats, is considered to be problem with cats of adult age.[31] It may be quite normal, if associated with young cats, as a result of being separated from mom too early. However, once the cat is of adult age it becomes an unusual problem. In other words wool chewing, or wool sucking, can be compared to a human child sucking her thumb. The cat will usually prefer wool, i.e. knitted garments rather than raw wool, but if not available will try to satisfy her craving with synthetic fibers or cottons. Rather than the expected result of a nutritional deficiency, the chewing seems to be a craving for the actual fiber.[32] As cats age they need more fiber in their diet so, if your cat is chewing on wool, she may be trying to tell you that she needs a diet higher in fiber, more than the one she's presently eating. If the diet change doesn't entirely clear up her problem it has been suggested to try her on uncooked chicken wings[33] (remember, the cat also chews the bones of her prey). It is the chicken's leg bones that are a no-no - they are too brittle for proper ingestion. Look to make sure your cat is chewing on the wool, if not she may just be nuzzling it and you can offer her a wool sock of her own.

Houseplant eating, and or digging, can also be a real problem. It generally is related to two things, the normal craving for grass and the normal instinct to dig. Cats, in the wild, have plenty of access to plants and grass, while the indoor cat is restricted from these natural food sources. And, although carpets are nice, there is an apparent desire for a good roll in fresh dirt. Unfortunately cats can't always determine what houseplant is good for them and what one might be poisonous. The best thing you could do for her is to provide her access to her own outside area with lots of fresh dirt and edible plants. However, since that is impossible, in most cases, you might want to pay your local pet shop a visit for some cat grass, or other greenery, especially suited for indoor nibbling. You should also move, or restrict, her from the bothered houseplants. If you cannot move the houseplants you might try dusting them with cayenne pepper or ginger. Spray the leaves with a mister first so the substance will stick. I've used both, at different times, and they work equally well.

Pica, another eating disorder, is most commonly associated with the eating of cat litter, usually the clay variety. If you have just changed to a new litter you might catch your cat 'checking it out'. Cats will often smell and taste new things. Pica is almost always brought on by a stressful situation,[34] but can also be caused by a form of anemia.[35] If your cat is not stressed, but exhibits pica, you should have her tested for feline leukemia, as it is often associated with a pica-like appetite.[36]

FOOD ALLERGIES

Although not true eating disorders, they are disorders resulting from eating. Older cats may become sensitive to certain food ingredients. The digestive system just can't handle them and the results may be vomiting or very colorful diarrhea. Other displays of food allergies are patchy coat and red itchy bumps. But, vomiting and diarrhea are the most dangerous for the older cats, as they may become dehydrated. I've noticed that foods containing red and yellow dyes, even tolerated when younger, may produce severe allergic-like reactions in my older cats. Also, if their diet is changed too often allergies may result. If the allergic reaction is very severe you should seek advice from your veterinarian.

SUPPLEMENTS

During your cat's life there are specific stages that have different nutritional requirements. When your cat was a kitten she needed high protein and high calorie diets to promote growth and energy. When she was carrying and raising kittens she needed high calorie foods for good energy to keep her body healthy. As an adult she could get by with reduced protein, because of reduced activity. Now, as an older adult, she may require supplements to help her handle diseases, i.e. kidney- liver- , heart- and intestinal-related, associated with old age. You need to know what to give her and when to give it. If supplements are necessary they may be of great benefit, if not they may even be harmful. Good candidates for diet supplementation would be cats on home-prepared diets, cats that refuse to eat and cats with specific diagnosed medical problems. As in any special diet, always consult your veterinarian before giving supplements.

Cats fed home-prepared diets may have calcium deficiencies. All meat diets, i.e. liver or fish, especially de-boned, can be low in calcium, but high in phosphorus. But before you put down an extra dish of milk to supplement calcium, you need to know that calcium and phosphorus need to be in the proper amounts to be able to work together. If not in correct amounts the phosphorus can actually destroy the calcium, giving you more problems.[37] Also some older cats cannot digest the lactose in the milk and will come down with diarrhea, another debilating problem for the older cat. If you prepare your cat's diet it's always advisable to check with your veterinarian to make sure it is nutritionally balanced.

Older cats may seem to lose their interest in food. This can be attributed to diminishing sense of smell. Although they don't require smell to be able to eat, it appears much more enjoyable for them to be able to smell their food.[38] You might want to try flavor enhancers such as garlic or onion powders, just a little, to stimulate appetite. Heating the food may also enhance both odor and flavor. If that doesn't work, check with your veterinarian about nutritional supplementation to stimulate her appetite. There is a 'trick of the trade' that may be beneficial - a little vegetable oil. In this case, a little really goes a long way. Try adding a tablespoon to her regular food once a week. It will not only keep her skin and coat healthy, aid in passing the hairball buildup, but she may also like it.[39]

Many older cats develop diseases linked to protein requirements. Probably the most common, of these diseases, is kidney disease. Cats developing kidney disease require a lower amount of protein, to alleviate extra stress on the kidneys. If your cat has kidney disease she may not be too interested in eating and may require appetite stimulants, as prescribed by your veterinarian.

Protein deficiency signs include a dull, sparse coat and susceptibility to respiratory problems.[40] Over a long period of time other signs will include weight loss and low blood protein.[41] One of the most supplemented proteins is the amino acid taurine. In the 1980s it was confirmed that the taurine content was insufficient in manufactured cat foods. Since that time manufacturers have added the adequate required amount. Cats with a taurine deficiency often displayed a heart disease, dilated cardiomyopathy, which could be fatal if the cat was not supplemented with taurine. According to studies, over the past 20 years, at the University of Calif. at Davis, a form of retinal degeneration leading to blindness can also be prevented by supplementing taurine.[42] This is definitely food for thought. Cats fed 'people-food' diets may develop fatty acid deficiency. Signs of this deficiency include fine dandruff, a dry, dull coat and itching.[43] Adding lecithin, a naturally occurring fatty acid, one teaspoon of granules daily, to the diet may help. You might also try butter, or margarine®, licked off your finger. Your cat may just give you an extra lick for it.

The last supplement an older cat may require is potassium. Potassium is important for electrolyte balance and proper muscle function.[44] Electrolytes are the substances in your cat's body that give her extra energy. When your cat loses body fluids, such as in kidney disease or severe diarrhea, these electrolytes are lost and she becomes weak. A good source of electrolyte replacement is Pedialite.® A little Pedialite® in her drinking water or mixed in her food daily works wonders.[45]

CHOOSING THE RIGHT DIET

If there was only one cat food available this choice would be easy. However, there are many manufacturers, each with many styles of food to choose from. You must consider your lifestyle; the type of food best suited, the nutritional quality of the food chosen, and - will your cat like it?

In the United States there are three basic forms of cat food to choose from: dry, semi-moist, and moist or canned food. Each has advantages and disadvantages. Of the brands, most easily accessible at the stores, most are comparable in nutrition.

They vary a little in amounts of protein and fats but not too differently. Some are more brightly colored than others, which is for our appeal rather than our cats. Basically, they are all healthful and up to required standards. If your cat has special diet needs, it's best to buy your cat's food through your veterinarian. If you have professional needs you should probably buy from a feed store or pet supply warehouse.

Choose the type of food geared best for your life style. For example, dry food can be put down and left out all day, while you're at work, for your cat to nibble on. Moist food, although good first thing in the morning, will spoil and become hard by midday. Likewise semi-moist, if not eaten immediately, will become hard.

Once you've decided what type of food you wish to serve your cat, you need to choose the best food possible. Compare labels from different manufacturers. Be sure to choose a sufficient fat and protein level. Also look at the fiber content. Whatever food you choose should be marked as 'complete and balanced nutrition', somewhere on the can, box or bag.

Your cat, herself, also needs to have a 'say' in the food decision. Older cats frequently have trouble with their teeth. Look at your cat's teeth. Dry food will help keep her teeth cleaner, but if she has few or broken teeth you should consider something softer. Texture and shape of the food seems to be important to older cats, too. My older cats seem to prefer the star shapes rather than the ball-shaped food. Flavor, for the older cat, is probably most important. In canned foods each manufacturer has quite a selection of flavors to choose from. I think a little variety adds spice to their lives and keeps mealtimes interesting.

FEEDING

Feeding also depends on your lifestyle. If you work, during the day, you should leave something down for your cat to nibble on. This free feeding may keep her from being bored, and she'll get a little exercise as well. If your cat is overweight, of course, free feeding will not work out for her. Two small meals a day, while you're there to monitor her food intake is much better. If you're home most of the time, and your cat is on the thin side, you might try four or five meals a day. I'm in and out all day long so, I feed my house cats canned food in the mornings and leave dry food down for free feeding. Plenty of clean water should be available at all times, especially when free feeding dry food.

You may notice your older cat turning her nose up at her regular food occasionally. It is a commonly known fact that older cats may become finicky eaters. As your cat ages, her senses of smell and taste diminish. A little garlic or onion powder may bring out the food's flavor and make it tasty for her again. Stay away from adding table salt, it does enhance flavor for us humans but it can be dangerous for your cat, especially one with weakening kidneys. You might also try adding small amounts of cheese, cooked eggs, tuna fish or cottage cheese and baby food. Warmed hot dogs, cut into small pieces, or warm chicken broth should also peak her interest. Check your local market for cat treats. My oldest house cats love extra treats. The already prepared cat treats are much better for them, than saving table scraps. At least you know the treats are nutritionally all right.

LAST WORDS ON DIET

Basically, the older cat needs: an adequate amount of protein, adjusted to her lifestyle activity; low carbohydrates, but medium to high fiber content; moderate fat, for good skin and shiny coat, and it all must be in a tasty and easily digestible form. Watch out for allergic reactions to cat foods. Colorful diarrhea can be uncomfortable as well as unhealthy for your older cat. If you add eggs to her diet, always cook them first. Raw eggs will cause her to become deficient in biotin, a much needed vitamin. Before making any changes in her normal diet, please, check with your veterinarian. There are several things in our favor: the better the food you feed, the more it's utilized by your cat, the less litter box cleaning you'll have to do. The healthier she is the less visits to your veterinarian.

After you have considered all the facts on proper diet, there is one rule of thumb you need to know about old cats eating, that is: To keep them eating, and do anything you have to do to accomplish this. My oldest cat Felix, 19 years, enjoys a donut in the mornings. At this time it is the French style donut that he particularly enjoys. And, he really enjoys eating it. He may know something about eating habits that I don't, in any event it gives me pleasure to see him still enjoying his food.

Photo by J. Lindley

One of my favorite felines, Felix, enjoying his favorite morning snack.

DIET NOTES

[1] *June Kirvan-Tuttle and Mark L. Morris Jr., Feline Nutrition, The Cornell Book of Cats (N.Y.: Villard Books d. of Random House 1992): 71.*

[2] *Gary Brodsky, The Mind of the Cat (Secaucus, N.J.: Castle Books): 67.*

[3] *"Your Cat's Diet", Catnip a Newsletter of Tufts Univ. (Nov.1995): 1.*

[4] *Francis A. Kallfelz, "Choosing the Best Diet", Cat Fancy Magazine (April 1991): 54.*

[5] *Checking canned cat food labels.*

[6] *Purina News Service 10/95, Ralston Purina.*

[7] *"Your Cat's Diet", Catnip a Newsletter of Tufts Univ. (Nov.1995): 2.*

[8] *June Kirvan-Tuttle and Mark L. Morris Jr., Feline Nutrition, The Cornell Book of Cats (N.Y.: Villard Book- d. Random House 1992): 73.*

[9] *ibid.*

[10] *ibid.*

[11] *"Discovering the Benefits of Dietary Fiber" Purina News Service, Ralston-Purina (6/95).*

[12] *"Pet Nutrition Terms Defined", Purina News Service, Ralston-Purina (10/95).*

[13] *ibid.*

[14] *ibid.*

[15] *June Kirvan-Tuttle and Mark L. Morris Jr., Feline Nutrition, The Cornell Book of Cats (N.Y.: Villard Books div. of Random House1992): 74.*

[16] *ibid: pg 78.*

[17] *Personal observations J. Lindley.*

[18] *Mark L. Morris Jr. and June Kirvan- Tuttle. Diseases of Dietary Origin, The Cornell Book of Cats (N.Y.: Villard Books, div. of Random House 1992): 86.*

[19] *ibid.*

[20] *Personal observations - J. Lindley.*

[21] *ibid.*

[22] *Cornell's Animal Health Newsletter (Mar. 1995): 3.*

[23] *ibid.*

[24] *ibid: 4.*

[25] *Dr. Biourge. Cornell's Animal Health Newsletter, (Mar, 1995): 4.*

[26] *Cornell's Animal Health Newsletter, (Mar. 1995): 4.*

[27] *June Kirvan-Tuttle, Jeffrey E. Barlough, Mordecai Siegal and Leo A. Wuori, Aging Cats and Disorders, The Cornell Book of Cats (N.Y.: Villard Books d. Random House 1992): 310.*

[28] *Personal observations J. Lindley.*

[29] *Personal observations J. Lindley.*

[30] *Personal observations J. Lindley.*

[31] *Katherine A. Houpt, Feline Behavior, The Cornell Book of Cats (N.Y.: Villard Books d. Random House 1992): 67.*

[32] *Personal observations - J. Lindley.*

[33] *Catnip, Newsletter of Tuft's Univ (July 1993): 8.*

[34] *Cornell's Animal Health Newsletter (June 1987): 3.*

[35] *ibid.*

[36] *Lennox M. Ryland, Cornell's Animal Health Newsletter (June 1987): 3.*

[37] *Francis A. Kallfelz, "Nutritional Deficiencies In Cats", Cat Fancy Magazine (April 1991): 26.*

[38] *Personal observations - J. Lindley.*

[39] *ibid.*

[40] *Francis A. Kallfelz, "Nutritional Deficiencies In Cats", Cat Fancy Magazine (April 1991): 26.*

[41] *ibid.*

[42] *Margaret Reister, "Good Nutrition Shines Through", Cat Fancy Magazine (May 1995): 10.*

[43] *ibid.*

[44] *June Kirvan-Tuttle, Mark L. Morris Jr., Feline Nutrition, The Cornell Book of Cats (N.Y.: Villard Books 1992): 75.*

[45] *Personal observations J. Lindley.*

4. CREATURE COMFORTS

We all want to be comfortable in our old age and our companion cats should be no exceptions. In the case of the older cat comfort is what makes anything easier for them, whether it is softer beds, cat posts, toys or special treats. These items of comfort can be found in pet stores, department stores, some grocery stores, and, for those of you who wish to shop at home, there are many pet catalogs, and of course on-line shopping. The magazine, Catster, features Marketplaces for cat supplies, as well as great articles of health and care interest. Since people are becoming pet aware the pet supplies are much more numerous than ever before. You just need to choose what's right for your cat.

BEDS

Since older cats spend up to 80% of their time sleeping, where they rest is important. Wait! Before you rush out to buy the fanciest bed available, check in what position your cat sleeps most often. In the warm months, my older cats sleep stretched out. Some on their backs, with belly-side up, others on their sides. In the colder months, they either curl together in the dog's bed or separately in cardboard boxes. (The cardboard holds in body heat.) For cats that lie in stretched out positions pads work best. For curling cats try the cup shaped fleece lined beds. Foam padding, and egg-crate foam, can be cut into a variety of sizes and shapes and when covered with a washable blanket or towel, make a most suitable bed. For the cold nights you can even add an electric heating pad, set on low. Other pads you might consider are a polyester fiber pad, called a Purr Pad®. My old cats really appreciated these, last winter. The Purr Pad® acts as an insulator to absorb and hold heat, as well as traps dirt, dust and hair. I used one in my (our) favorite bedroom chair. The cats loved it and the pad protected the chair seat as well. It is definitely a worthwhile product. For real pampered comfort you might even be interested in a feline waterbed. According to the manufacturer, they are wood framed and come with U-L approved heaters, heavy duty liners and durable, washable, quilted covers to protect the mattress. What more could a pampered older cat want?

SWEATERS AND BLANKETS

The majority of older cats get thin with age. They lose the upper layer of body fat that would normally keep them warm. When they are normally moving around the house, especially during cold months, they may need an extra layer of warmth. My cat, Felix, who's rapidly approaching nineteen, sports a bright red and purple sweater.

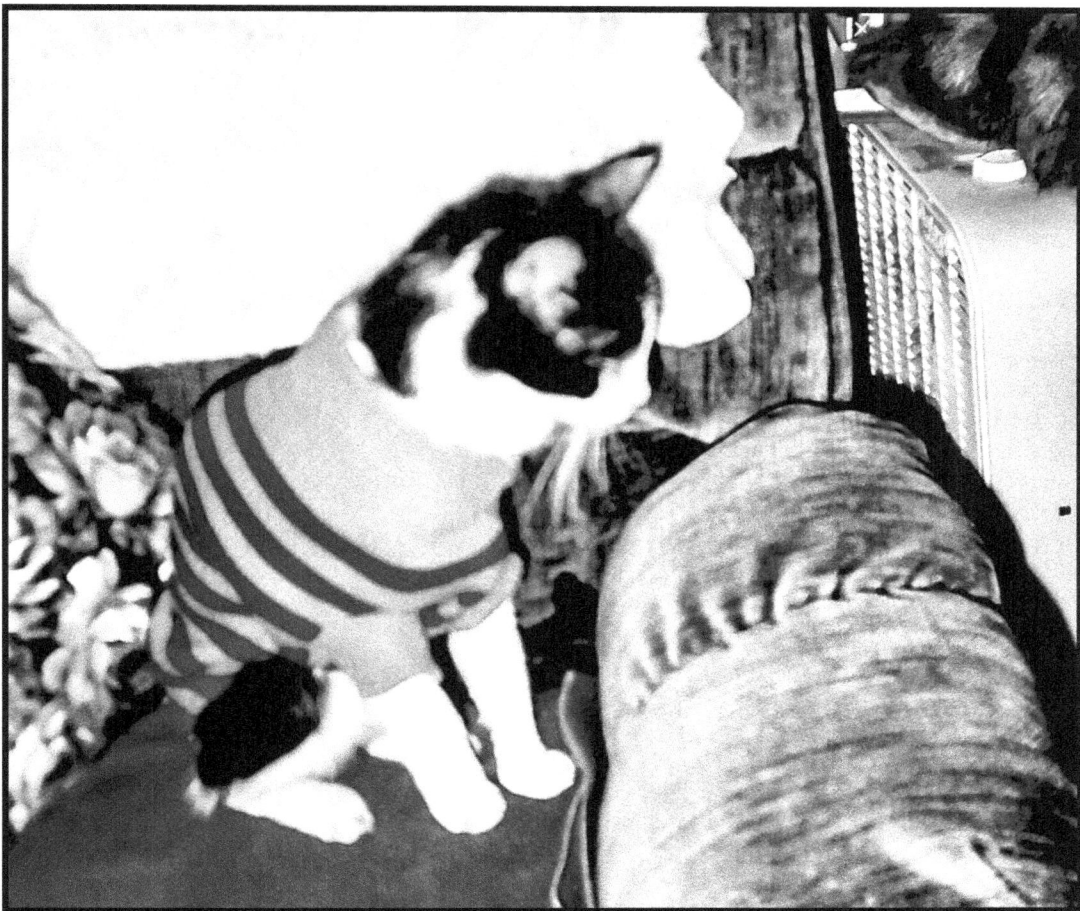

Photo by J. Lindley

Felix (almost 19) feels the need of a sweater. He actually won't give it up without a fight.

The first few times I put it on him there was quite a hassle. Now, as soon as it gets cold he sits by it and meows until it's put on. With his sweater on he may sleep anywhere, without it he's found only in front of the heater. Although some cats may find sweaters too restricting, Felix really likes his.

Blankets and throws are also things you need to have plenty of for the older cat. The pet catalogs offer a wide selection of washable blankets and throws, some with black paw prints already on them. These are not only great for the comfort of our cats, but will also protect our furniture. Whether they are hand-made or store-bought, they are quite warm and very comfortable to have around during cold months.

CAT POSTS AND OTHER SCRATCHERS

Cat posts serve two purposes to your older cat, a scratching surface and a hiding place. Your older cat needs to be able to scratch on a regular basis. Scratching not only helps her remove the claw covering but also exercises her toe muscles. The claw coverings may become thicker with age and removing them is difficult for your older cat. Sometimes I see mine grab the claw with their teeth and pull off the covering. Scratching is much easier for them and probably more enjoyable. Unless you prefer your cat to use your furniture for this purpose, you should provide a sturdy cat post. Coverings may vary, according to manufacturer, so you need to choose one acceptable to your cat. Favored scratching surfaces are carpet (20% favored), upholstered fabric (20%) wood, (20%), followed by sisal (11%) and corrugated cardboard (9%) then miscellaneous surfaces.[1] No wonder they like couches. The manufacturers, of cat posts, offer most of these surfaces, sometimes even in combinations. Elaborate cat posts are available with perches and hiding holes as well as the proper desired scratching surfaces. However, since the risk of injury due to falling is greater with senior cats, you may want to keep the height to a minimum.

Corrugated cardboard surfaces are featured in both flat pads as well as in combination with toys. They, too, are great surfaces for claw cover pulling. If you cannot find one, try making one. Cut a corrugated cardboard box into strips, about 1½ inches wide, place on the narrow side, with holes up, and tie, with string, into a bundle. My cats enjoy shredding their cardboard immensely.

TOYS

Toys for the older cat should be the type that encourages exercise. String toys, including those with feathers, to wiggle or dangle work well. My cats even enjoy a shoelace dragged around for them to chase. A sewing spool and string makes an interesting toy and provides hours of fun. Whether your cat swats or chases the toy, the exercise is beneficial for her good circulation and slowing muscles. Quieter toys, those of self-interest, include the stuffed pillow type or catnip mouse variety. Many old cats like stuffed animals to roll around, or curl up, with.

CATNIP

Whether in a toy, or offered by itself (dry or fresh) it is a treat and toy combined - and will definitely spark up your oldster's life. They say the sense of smell diminishes with age but with the added enhancement, by the use of the Jacobsen's Organ (see Nose, Capt. II) your cat may still enjoy catnip very much. Catnip contains nepetalactone, a hallucinogenic chemical substance that induces a pleasure response.[2] No wonder they roll around and look drunk - they are.

Fresh or dried, catnip can be purchased or even home grown. The taste for catnip is inherited, with 60% to 70% of adult cats responding to some degree.[3] A really sensitive cat can detect the volatile oil of catnip at an atmospheric concentration of one part per billion.[4] Of course, there is more oil in fresh catnip than in dry, but both seem to be most satisfactory to the older cat.[5]

Catnip, nepeta cataria, also known as catmint is extremely hardy. If you decide to grow it, be sure to limit its growing space. I made the mistake of planting it with spearmint equally in a flower box. The catnip eagerly took over and the poor spearmint was relegated to the far end of the box. I have now limited the catnip to its own flower pot. It has survived both our summer heat and winter frost with little damage. It will tolerate sun but seems to prefer partial shade and it likes lots of water. It would also make a great houseplant, for one cat to nibble on, at her leisure. I'm afraid if I grew it in my house it would be attacked too often by too many. I remember, my grandmother grew both mint and catnip near her backdoor. My great grandmother took catnip, brewed, as tea every night to help her sleep. I have catnip tea also to calm myself, but it hasn't the same effect on me that it does on my cats. They really enjoy their spice-of-life, the catnip.

LITTER and LITTER BOXES

These are not exactly comfort items, but if not right, they are definitely uncomfortable items, for both you and your cat. There are quite a variety of cat litters offered at the stores. They range in styles of coarse clays to fine clay, clumping litters, as well as alfalfa-, wheat- and wood-based litters. Whichever you choose should be suited to your cat, otherwise she won't use the box. I tried the green, alfalfa-based, litter once, and my house cats thought it was something to eat. For my cats in the retirement buildings, I use the clumping litter. It's soft, less tracked, very absorbent, and controls odors well. Best of all, they like it.

Another problem I had with finding the 'correct' litter was scent. It almost goes without saying, that we would all like to cover up the odor produced by the box. Unfortunately my older cats didn't like the heavily scented litters. And, to really show their disapproval, they did their business just outside the box. One of my older girls tried to use it, but had sneezing fits when she scratched in it. So, it's back to square one. I did find that mixing a little baking soda in with the litter helped with the odor and was not rejected by the cats.

The style of litter box can also be as important as what it holds. In my multi-cat house I offer a variety of litter boxes, some are covered, some with a side guard and some regular, uncovered boxes. Some boxes have high sides, to accommodate litter throwers, and some have lower sides. All boxes apparently get used as I clean them often. Box position is also important. The majority of my cats use the boxes in their own special room - so they must like privacy. Regarding privacy, there are privacy screens to go around the discriminating cat's litter box.

COMPANIONS

Comfort for the older cat is not always something that can be purchased for her. Some older cats need more companionship than even you can provide. They need a special friend. Adding a new cat to your house might be just what the doctor ordered for an older cat. But before you rush out to rescue, or adopt one, there are things to be considered. How old is your cat? How high is her energy level tolerance? Will she even accept a friend? The best, and only, way to find out is to make the attempt. Take a new cat on a 'lease-option-to-own' basis. That way she can be returned if the friendship isn't realized. If your cat is really old she may feel like she is being replaced and reject a new friend entirely. On the other hand, I have seen a young kitten come into the life of an oldster and really brighten it up.

The energy level is a prime concern. Cats of advanced age get tired quicker, and then get grouchy. In that case, a young cat, say between 1 yr - 3 yrs, might be the best bet. I have a handicapped kitten, Sunny Monster, who keeps my house oldsters on their toes. She holds her right front paw up, as she was stepped on by a horse, thus limiting her activity somewhat. Being young, she still plays and pesters the oldsters just enough to keep their lives interesting. She's a real blessing, as well as a comfort to those of us who love her.

SPECIAL CARE KITTIES

Cats with debilitating diseases, amputations and arthritis require and deserve special care. Sometimes it's hard to decide how much pain they are actually in. I believe it is evidenced by their normal activity. As long as the cat shows interest in life and moves around, even a severely arthritic one, I will try to make her comfortable. Special care kitties often have a difficult time deciding how they wish to rest. Cats suffering from mild to severe arthritis sleep in a stomach down position, with head resting on front legs or paws. In most cases, they are unable to rest in the normal curled position since arthritis usually affects the hip joints and back. All special kitties require a softer, deeper padded bed, soft blankets and, during cold months, an electric heating pad. Other considerations are lower litter box sides, (or one side trimmed down with a door) and minimal exercise. You may substitute a gentle brushing and holding time for playtime. Be sure to check her claws as an arthritic or otherwise physically challenged, cat can't tend to their own claw covering pulling. If she can't jump up to her favorite sleeping spot, you might provide her a stool, or a ramp. A large soft floor pillow can be of great comfort. You may also need to move her litter box, food and water dishes closer to her normal sleeping area. If your arthritic cat seems unusually stiff necked you may elevate her food and water dishes a little. Remember the best comfort you can give your special cat is your understanding and love.

CREATURE COMFORTS - NOTES

[1] *Audry Pavia, "Damage Control", Cat Fancy Magazine (June 1996): 36.*

[2] *"Catnip: Kitty's Delight", Catnip, Newsletter of Tufts Univ. School of Vet. Med. (Vol. 1 No. 2 1993): 8.*

[3] *Wendy Christensen, "Crazy For Catnip", Cat Fancy Magazine (May 1994): 19.*

[4] *ibid: pg 18.*

[5] *Personal observations - J. Lindley.*

TRAVEL CARE

America has been called the Country on Wheels. Summer vacations have always been a part of our lives. When I was younger, my parents went away for a short vacation every summer. Until I was seventeen, I went with them. Of course our family dog went along too. Dogs behave and come when they're called, so there is not too many problems with them getting too far away when you let them out of your vehicle. They can also be tethered with food and water available, for long durations. It's not as easy traveling with a cat, unless you have an air conditioned motor home. It's not as comfortable for the cat either.

There are several things you need to consider before you decide whether or not your cat is going with you. Many older cats stress very easily and changing environments is a chief cause of stress. On the other hand older cats can suffer separation anxiety easily. Separation anxiety is your cat's personal response to your being gone for a prolonged period of time. So, what to do? Hopefully the information in this chapter will help you make the right decisions for your cat's comfort and your own as well.

One last note, anytime you travel with your cat, or leave her in another's care, you should make sure you have all her health information available. If you are traveling with a permanent end destination, rather than a turn around vacation, you may want to check ahead to see what shots might be required there. For example rabies vaccinations are required for cats in the eastern states. A health certificate from your veterinarian is a small price to pay, for the enjoyment of having your cat accompany you on your trip.

1. TRAVELING WITH YOUR CAT

So, you're planning a trip and you can't bear the thought of leaving your old cat behind. Traveling with your cat can be enjoyable for both of you as long as it's done safely.

In 1986 it was necessary for my family to make a trip across the United States, from California to Maine. We actually only got as far as Colorado and had to make repairs to our vehicle then return home. At that time my family consisted of my husband, three young children and myself. My animal family however was quite numerous, ten house cats, about forty cattery cats, and nine dogs. My oldest house cat, Grayless, had suffered separation anxiety, by refusing to eat, when she was younger, so even though she was eighteen years old I decided to take her with me. We also took three of the dogs along to help guard the vehicles. Leaving all the other animals behind was very hard for me but I did have someone there to take care of them. We traveled in a family caravan of three buses and two vans, with my oldest daughter and her husband in one bus and his brother and his family in another bus. We alternated drivers in the vans. All in all it was a rather eventful summer vacation. The intention was to travel straight through to Maine, work on a friend's saw mill, then return home in time for school. It didn't work out that way. We got as far as Colorado; one bus went home after a week, our bus stayed for an extra month while being repaired, and my daughter's bus stayed until December. Fortunately, although it was eventful for us, humans, Grayless came through the entire trip with very few problems.

I was very glad that I took her, she was great comfort at night, when I seemed to worry about the others left behind more. I did pick up some interesting tips while on the journey. Grayless was confined to a large cat carrier, with litter box and water, and food, during the day when we traveled. The carrier was strapped in place so that it wouldn't jar around, or become airborne should we be involved in an accident. I checked her water often throughout the day. Since senior cats can be easily affected by water changes I used only bottled water. I did encounter one problem I wasn't expecting, Grayless was use to canned food in the mornings but if I fed it the days we moved she had motion sickness. I'd never given a thought about a cat having motion sickness. So, the days we traveled, Grayless had her dry food to nibble on. When we stopped, and over night, Grayless was allowed out but only after the windows were checked. She taught me a lot that trip, what an older cat can tolerate and a great lesson in patience. I never regretted taking her with me and she actually seemed to enjoy the trip as well.

Traveling in your own bus is one thing, traveling by car is a very different thing. Before you leave home carefully plan your itinerary for stays at 'cat friendly' places and be sure you pack for your cat's comfort as well as her basic needs. Take your own water from home or use bottled water to prevent intestinal discomfort.

Since cats are now considered as America's #1 companion animal, and more cats are accompanying their owners, many hotels and motels accept them as guests, but it's always best to phone first.

For the comfort of your cat, while traveling, be sure to have her carrier large enough to move around in. Even though she's old, she still needs to stretch her tired bones a bit, especially if it's in more than two hour intervals. It's also nice to have the carrier large enough for a small litter pan and food and water dishes. Your cat may travel more calmly if she has a favorite toy, blanket, towel or an article of clothes, with your scent on it, with her. Also the car radio, tuned to a 'mood music' station, will help keep her calm. Remember to check her water often. And, never leave your cat shut in a car with the windows up. Cars can get hot very quickly and it could cause heat stroke in a very short time. Your cat should wear a breakaway collar with her I.D. on it, just in case an escape occurs. If your cat objects to traveling in her carrier, especially for a prolonged time, you might want to consider a seat belt for her. The seat belt would allow her a bit more moving space and she could look out the window, should she desire to do so. If you travel in the heat, you might offer your cat a frozen bottle of water, or a blue ice pack under a towel liner.

For staying in motels (or hotels) I've found it's helpful to provide a scratching pad. There are many types available, but my cats preferred the fold out cardboard or the carpeted door knob hanging ones. Clumping litters work best for traveling as they don't track too much and they're easier to vacuum up. If your cat has a few toys with her she should not become too bored. Sometimes boredom can equal destruction, especially with an already stressed cat in unfamiliar surroundings. Being a good motel guest not only will allow her a return visit, but will make it easier for the next cat to visit. If you are a AAA member, log onto their website, they have lists of pet friendly hotels and motels.

Cleo (14) and Laska (16) under cover, traveled all over Europe and Central America with Charlotte Miller, nowadays of Coeur D'Alene, ID.

Peaches Cee traveled to Alaska and back with his lady, Helen Cloutier
of Hacienda Heights, Calif. Peaches is now 16 ½ years old.

2. TRAVELING WITHOUT YOUR CAT

If you need to make a trip and you can't take your cat, or you think it might
be too stressful for her, there are still many things to consider, for her comfort while
you're away. In most circumstances, if you are going to be away only for a day or two,
it's safe to leave food and water down for her, as well as a clean litter box. Double
check your windows and be sure to alert a neighbor in case of a problem. If there are
special circumstances, such as special food or medical problems, you might need to
consider boarding her with your veterinarian. Should you need to be away for a longer
period, a professional Pet Sitter might be advisable. A reliable, and bonded, Pet Sitter
who comes in to check on a regular basis and your cat's own familiar surroundings
is much better for her than a boarding kennel situation. You may also check with

your veterinarian for a referral to a reliable pet-caring person. Before you leave be sure to write down all pertinent information, such as feeding instructions, potential medical problems and emergency care numbers. You should also provide, if possible, phone numbers where you could be contacted should a problem arise. If you have questions, or feel uncomfortable with care, ask about it before you leave. Don't leave your baby without knowing she'll be properly cared for. If you're to be gone for more than a week, call in and speak to your cat, that way she'll know you still care, and it will ease her separation anxiety. If you can't be there in person at least you can still "reach out and touch" her.

3. TRAVEL BY AIRLINE

In 1969 I traveled with Grayless and Stokley, her brother, by air. In those days cats were held in the baggage compartment during the flight. Fortunately it was a short flight, from Los Angeles, Calif. to Salt Lake City, Utah, as I worried about them all the way. Baggage compartments, then, were not air temperature controlled and sometimes with animals, particularly large dogs, there had been problems. Fortunately my two cats suffered no ill effects and were very happy to see me at the other end. I attribute this to two things, they were young cats and they had each other (in the same travel crate) for comfort.

First, and foremost, call around to the different air lines and see which ones allow pets and what the rates are, as regulations and requirements have changed. Even with flying made easier for cats, nowadays, it should be remembered that cats are very nervous creatures and keenly aware of what goes on around them, but the older ones can't cope with stressful situations as well as the younger ones. Be sure to be there for your cat, an airplane terminal can be awfully confusing for her, and even for people.

In 1995 it was estimated that some 500,000 cats and dogs fly annually,[1] and I'm sure that it's higher by now. There are occasions, such as a cross country move, when your cat will be traveling with you. It's always much better if we can fly with them in a carrier under the seat, but sometimes that's not an option. Unless your cat has traveled, by air, alone before this type of travel can be very upsetting, and confusing, especially for an older cat. She may refuse to eat, or drink, and meow loudly, to show her unhappiness. Should she require tranquilizers, for air travel, please check with her veterinarian first. Make sure your cat has a regulation airline carrier that has sufficient moving around room and attached water/food dishes. An article of clothing, with your scent on it, and toys, blanket or towel should be a comfort for her. Many airlines require health certificates, issued no more than 10 days prior to trip, attached to the carrier, as well as I.D. (including the destination). It's a comforting thought that the United States Department of Agriculture oversees the handling of animals that travel out of their owner's custody.[2] But, it's always advisable to check with the airline and request your cat be checked on periodically. Be sure to have her met promptly at her destination.

NOTES

[1] *Estimated by the Air Transport Association of America, "Travel Tips for Pet Passengers" Joe Dziemianowicz, Cats Magazine (June 1995): 31.*

[2] *ibid: pg 32.*

HEALTH CARE

We all want to do what's best for our old cats, when they're not feeling well, we just need to know what to do and when to do it. Subjects included in this section will help you to recognize the major disease symptoms, if first aid is applicable and what is an emergency situation. Also included are discussions on anesthesia risks, recuperative care, pain management, and alternate remedies. Some of this information is already scattered throughout this book but the importance indicates necessity of a section of its own.

1. DISEASES MOST COMMON TO OLDER CATS

Disease/Disorder	Cause	Symptoms	Treatment
1. Kidney Disease[1] Chronic Kidney Failure also Chronic Interstitial Nephritis Common in Cats Over 10 Years Old	aging, failing kidneys	refusal to eat, weight loss, depression, weakness, bad breath, mouth ulcers, increased thirst and urination, dehydration	Special Diet (low protein) potassium supplements, in severe cases: surgery
Chronic Renal Failure[2]	age	anemia, increased acidity and gastric ulcers, mouth ulcers and bad breath	Special Diet with restricted protein and potassium
2. Hyperthyroidism[3] The most common endocrine disorder in cats – A disease of middle-aged and older cats.	over production of the thyroid gland	weight loss, ravenous appetite, hyperactivity, restlessness, increased thirst and urination strong, rapid heart beat	drug therapy, surgery to remove thyroid gland and radioactive iodine therapy

Disease/Disorder	Cause	Symptoms	Treatment
3. Diabetes Mellitus Over Weight Cats More At Risk	lack of insulin output from pancreas	increased urination, increased amount of urine, inc. thirst, lethargy, inc. appetite but weight loss, rear leg weakness, diarrhea, vomiting, poss. loss of hair, mouth sores, cataracts, slow healing wounds	regimented insulin dosages and special diet
4. Heart Disease (dilated cardiomyopathy) Middle-aged and older cats cab be associated with hyperthyroidism	enlarged heart taurine deficiency	weak, tired, lack of appetite, edema (fluid in the lungs or stomach) enlarged heart chambers with weak walls	taurine supplements medication prescribed by veterinarian
5. Arthritis (osteoarthritis)	degenerating joint/deteriorating bone end cartilage – actual cause unknown	lameness, stiffness, sway-backed, refusal to move	minimum exercise, keep warm, no drafts, padded beds, check with your vet for pain relief
6. Cancer & Tumors Chance increases with age	some prone – some not cause unknown	unusual lumps, swellings, sores that won't heal	removal surgery radiation and and chemotherapy
7. Liver Disease[4] (hepatic lipidosis)	fat accumulation in liver cells result in short term starvation	refusal to eat, weight loss, lethargy, weakness, seizures, loss of motor control	stimulate appetite vitamin supplements forced feedings
(cirrhosis)	tissue degeneration and scarring	vomiting, lethargy, anorexia, neurologic dyfunction, watery diarrhea	Special Diet to slow down degeneration

Disease/Disorder	Cause	Symptoms	Treatment
8. Constipation Very common not usually serious	slowing digestive system	hard stools, straining, impaction	High fiber diet, stool softeners, butter licked from your finger will help

IF YOU SEE ANY OF THE ABOVE SYMPTOMS IN YOUR OLDER CAT, PLEASE SEE YOUR VETERINARIAN. IF DIAGNOSED AND TREATED SOON ENOUGH, YOUR CAT MAY STILL HAVE MANY GOOD YEARS AHEAD OF HER.

General Information from:

Cornell Book of Cats (N.Y.: Villard Books d. Random House 1992):

Circulatory System and Disorders pgs 193-194 (dilated cardiomyopathy) by N. Sydney Moise; Aging Cats & Disorders, pg. 309-314 Kidney, Liver and Heart Diseases, digestive system and tumors by June Kirvan-Tuttle, Jeffrey E. Barlough, Mordecai Siegal, and Leo A. Wuori; also, Musculoskeletal System and Disorders pg. 202 (osteoarthritis) by Jeffrey E. Barlough.

NOTES

1 *Amy Shojai, Health Handbook Kidney Failure, Cats Magazine (Sept. 1995):55.*
2 *Chronic renal failure and diabetes mellitus, Animal Health Newsletter, Cornell Univ. (Aug.1994):4.*
3 *Hyperthyroidism, Catnip Newsletter of Tufts Univ. School. of Vet Med (April 1994):l.*
4 *Hepatic Lipodosis, Animal Health Newsletter, Cornell Univ. (Oct.1993): 4.*

2. FIRST AID & OTHER EMERGENCY CARE

First aid is temporary aid to the injured, or ill, cat given to preserve life and alleviate suffering, or aggravation of the injury, until a veterinarian's service can be obtained. It requires the use of special techniques, and supplies in some cases. Emergency situations do not always require first aid, prior to transport, but may require special carrying procedures.

The first thing you must do is to remain calm. Most cats in pain are frightened and may lash out, or bite, even at you. Your gentle calm voice will go far in calming your cat.

Assess the situation, to determine what first aid procedure may be necessary. Give the appropriate first aid to the situation and transport, using proper carrying procedures, to your veterinarian. It is always wise to phone the veterinarian's office before you leave so they may prepare for your arrival.

Before I discuss first aid you need to know normal vital signs. Normal Rates[1] as follows:

- Pulse 160 - 240 per min.
- Breathing rate 20 - 30 per min.
- Temperature 100.4 - 102.5 degrees Fahrenheit

Anything abnormal may indicate problems and you should take your cat to her veterinarian as soon as possible.

First Aid supplies should always be on hand. You never know when you'll need them not only for your cat but maybe even for yourself. Suggested supplies are: 1 medium sized towel (or space blanket), various sizes of sterile gauze pads, roll of gauze bandage (one inch wide is the best), cotton roll or cotton balls, adhesive tape, antiseptic (i.e. hydrogen peroxide), antibiotic ointment, rectal thermometer, small scissors and tweezers. Also, have on hand your cat carrier for easy and safe transport.

Situations requiring first aid are: abnormal breathing (including choking); injuries (bleeding, non-bleeding, broken bones, sprains and internal), shock, heatstroke, poisoning, insulin shock, and sometimes bee, or other insect stings.[2]

ABNORMAL BREATHING

Without breath there is no life. Abnormal breathing covers differences in breathing patterns from slightly abnormal to not breathing and the need for mouth to mouth resuscitation. No matter what the cause, it is important to get your cat breathing normally again. Her normal breathing rate is determined by counting chest risings (inhalations) or fallings (exhalations), but not both. Changes in normal breathing rates indicate serious problems. Labored breathing indicates a possible obstruction; rapid breathing, possible shock or lack of oxygen; shallow breathing, a sign of weakness or chest pain; and irregular breathing may indicate fractured ribs, punctured or collapsed lung.[3] Other signs of respiratory distress are: pale or blue mucous membranes (gums); gasping or open-mouth breathing; and shallow breathing and unconscious with dilated eyes. If your cat shows any of these symptoms get her to her veterinarian immediately.

First aid may be necessary when an obstruction causes breathing difficulties such as gasping or choking. Choking is one of the signs of rabies[4] in cats, so if your cat is an outside cat and hasn't been vaccinated for rabies, call your veterinarian immediately. A choking cat may also paw at her mouth in an attempt to dislodge the object herself. To help your choking cat, you need to: 1. Restrain her by wrapping her in a towel, to prevent scratching; 2. Tilt her head back and open her mouth, to look in.; 3. If you can see the object, grasp it with tweezers to dislodge it; 4. If 3 fails, lay your cat on her side, place the heel of your hand just behind her last rib, angling slightly upward and push firmly. About four quick pushes should dislodge the object.[5] Be careful not to push so hard that you break her ribs. If this doesn't work get her to her veterinarian immediately.

If you find your cat not breathing, check for heart beat or pulse rate before applying first aid in the form of mouth-to-mouth resuscitation. You can feel her heart beat just below her ribs, or check her pulse rate by feeling the inside upper hind leg, where the femoral artery is. If she is not breathing apply mouth-to-mouth (actually mouth-to-nose) resuscitation as follows:

1. Clear her airway to remove any fluid by tilting her head down. Extend her head and neck to open airway and, if necessary clear with your finger. Pull her tongue forward.

2. Hold her mouth closed, place your mouth over her nose and mouth, and blow for 1 to 2 seconds until her chest expands. Blow gently to inflate her lungs. Wait 2 seconds and repeat until she's breathing on her own.

3. If there's no heart beat, try cardiac massage. Place your thumb on her chest behind her elbow, fingers on the other side of her chest. Gently squeeze at 2 compressions per second, until you feel a regular heart beat.[6]

INJURIES

Older cats frequently suffer injuries from falling off the tops of cabinets, or the refrigerator. My cat, Grayless, slipped off the refrigerator and sprained her back. She came down with a mild case of cystitis as a result of the abrupt landing. Since she was sixteen years old at the time, I rushed her to her veterinarian. He prescribed antibiotics and in a week or so she was her old self again. I was lucky. Falls can often have more serious results, such as broken bones, external bleeding or internal bleeding.

You should not attempt to splint broken bones. Leave that to the veterinarian. Try to make your cat comfortable, wrap her in a towel, put her in the carrier and transport her to her veterinarian. If she is bleeding, control the bleeding before transporting. Apply direct pressure to the wound with a sterile gauze pad. If it bleeds through, apply another pad on top. Do not remove the first pad, you may disturb a forming clot. If the bleeding does not stop, try applying pressure to the supplying arteries, to the area of the wound. Pressure points are inside upper front legs and hind legs also lower base of her tail. Very firm pressure should slow down the blood flow. If all else fails, apply a tourniquet. This is to be used as a last resort because there can be complications of gangrene, if not applied properly. Using one-inch wide gauze bandage, wrap twice around leg, or tail, between the wound and her body. Tie once, place a stick, or pencil, on top and tie a square knot. Twist slowly until the bleeding slows to a trickle. Fasten the stick in place with adhesive tape and cover wound with sterile gauze. The tourniquet should be released briefly every ten to fifteen minutes.

Signs of internal bleeding are bleeding from the mouth, ears, or anus, vomiting and/or defecating blood.[7] Internal bleeding can be very frightening because there's nothing to do for your cat, but keep her calm and get help as soon as possible.

Non-bleeding wounds, such as abrasions, can be received as a result of a fall, especially if it's a rug she lands on. To clean a non-bleeding wound: Cover the area around the wound with petroleum jelly, to prevent her hair from getting in; Clip her hair away from the wound; Wash with warm water then an antiseptic, ie. hydrogen peroxide; Using a wet cotton ball, or sterile gauze pad, clean the wound by gently washing from the center, of the wound, outward; blot away excess water; apply an antibiotic ointment; cover with a sterile gauze pad and bandage. The dressing should be changed every other day, to check healing. If the wound is deep enough to require stitches see your veterinarian. Anytime you notice an odd smell or unusual drainage, or the wound isn't healing properly, see your veterinarian.

SHOCK

Anytime there is loss of blood, or a severe injury, there is a chance of shock. To determine shock, check heart rate, pulse and breathing. Signs of shock are increased heart rate, rapid but weak pulse, rapid shallow breathing, pale gums, cold feel to body and sometimes the inability to stand as well as involuntary urination. If you determine your cat is in shock, keep her warm, hold her with her head lowered to promote flow of blood to her brain. Place her on her side, changing to the other side every 5 minutes, and get her to her veterinarian. Shock is very serious and can be fatal.[8]

HEATSTROKE

For those of us who live in very warm climates information on heatstroke is mandatory. Heatstroke, if not discovered in time can also be fatal. Signs of heatstroke are rapid breathing, panting, excessive salivating and vomiting. If your cat displays any of these symptoms, during the hot days of summer, she may be on the verge of heatstroke. Reduce her body temperature by wrapping her in cool wet towels. (I let my cats lie on wet towels during the summer heat) If she doesn't cool down, and becomes weak get veterinary help immediately.

POISONING

Poisoning is not too common in older cats, probably because they aren't quite as curious as younger cats. They don't often go exploring under the sink, where household cleaners are found and they usually have had their taste of bad plants by the time they're older. But, accidents do happen, once in awhile. Signs of poisoning can be salivating, swelling in the throat, sensitive areas in the mouth, vomiting, diarrhea, stomach pain, lethargy, staggering, twitching, convulsions and coma.[9] If you suspect that your cat has been poisoned, check for the possible cause and call the 24-Hour ASPCA National Animal Poison Control Center at 1-800-548-2423, or your veterinarian. If you know, describe what it was and how long ago your cat ingested it, as well as what signs she's displaying. Do not induce vomiting without consulting a professional first.[10]

INSULIN SHOCK

If your cat is being treated for diabetes an insulin shock can be a potential reality. When a cat has diabetes mellitus, insulin is given to suppress the sugar in the blood, and subsequently the urine. If an over dose of insulin is given, or if it is given on an empty stomach, your cat could possibly go into insulin shock. Most insulin shock reactions occur within a time range of between 2 to 6 hours, following the insulin injection. Signs of too much insulin are weakness, depression, excitability, salivation, seizures and loss of appetite. The best way to reverse these symptoms is to give your cat honey or sugar water orally. Since diabetic cats are pretty closely monitored by their veterinarians, your cat's veterinarian should be able to show you how to do this in advance of actual need.[11]

BEE AND OTHER INSECT STINGS

Older cats are pretty cautious around bees, as they may have encountered them before, so bee, or wasp, stings don't happen too often. Spider and ant bites might be more common. Bees don't often get into your house, but spiders and ants come a visiting, even where they are not wanted.

Depending on where (and by what) the sting is, your cat may have a problem. If your cat bites at a bee, she may be stung in her mouth and swelling will occur. If she is stung in the mouth she should be taken to her veterinarian. Cats often paw at spiders, or ants, and thus, get bitten on their paws. If the bite is between her paw pads, you might see a small red dot. Your cat will probably shake it and lick at it a lot. She may not want to put any weight on the paw. If she is in great discomfort, by all means, see the veterinarian. Otherwise, you might try a paste of baking soda and water, applied to the bite area. This should ease her pain and relieve itching. If you don't have baking soda, try a dab of calamine lotion.[12] It has the same soothing results. Generally, insect bites and bee stings cause relatively few problems. They are, mostly, just itchy. But if swelling occurs (ie. lips, eyelids or face) in the first 5 minutes, she may be having an allergic reaction and she should see her veterinarian right away.[13]

OTHER EMERGENCIES

There are other emergency situations that do not require first aid but do need quick medical attention. These situations are vomiting blood, blood in urine or stool, straining to urinate, or defecate, seizures and convulsions. In the case of seizures and convulsions you should wrap your cat in a towel, to keep her from hurting herself, and proceed to your veterinarian.

CARRYING PROCEDURES

In most cases the least amount of restraint the more your cat will be able to tolerate what is happening to her. If you find your cat in an unconscious state you should gently ease her on to a small blanket, or towel, and lift her into a box or carrier. If you use a regular cardboard box make sure the bottom is sturdy and cover the top with a heavy towel. This will help her feel more secure and calm, should she regain consciousness. If she's injured and conscious and you need to immobilize her wrap her in a towel, keeping her head out, then place her in her carrier. I have seen people use a pillow case to transport an injured or frightened cat. If you use a pillow case be sure to tie the end closed. The best and safest method of carrying is in a regular carrier designed for cats. You can also throw a towel over the cat carrier to calm your cat. Again, please remain calm, a speeding ticket only takes more time and time is very precious in an emergency.

FIRST AID NOTES

[1] *Robert W. Kirk and Mordecai Siegal, First Aid, The Cornell Book of Cats (N.Y.: Villard Books d. Random House 1992): 343.*

[2] *Robert W. Kirk and Mordecai Siegal, First Aid, The Cornell Book of Cats (N.Y.: Villard Books d. Random House 1992): 346.*

[3] *Robert W. Kirk and Mordecai Siegal, First Aid, The Cornell Book of Cats (N.Y.: Villard Books d. Random House 1992): 344.*

[4] *Robert W. Kirk and Mordecai Siegal, First Aid, The Cornell Book of Cats (N.Y.: Villard Books d. Random House 1992): 346.*

[5] *Choking procedure: ibid.*

[6] *Resuscitation procedure: The ABC's of Resuscitation, Catnip, newsletter of Tufts Univ. Sch. of Vet. Med. (Vol. 3, No. 9): 3.*

[7] *Robert W. Kirk and Mordecai Siegal, First Aid, The Cornell Book of Cats (N.Y.: Villard Books d. Random House 1992): 348.*

[8] *Shock, Catnip, Tufts Univ Sch of Vet. Med (Dec 1995): 2.*

[9] *Robert W. Kirk and Mordecai Siegal, Reference Guide: First Aid for Plant Poisoning, The Cornell Book of Cats. (N.Y.: Villard Books d. Random House 1992): 354-356.*

[10] *Poisoning, Catnip, Tufts Univ Sch. of Vet Med (Vol 3, No. 9): 3.*

[11] *Insulin Shock - verified by J. L. Woodring DVM.*

[12] *Calamine lotion - Dr. Larry Thompson, Cornell Univ. Insect Bites and Stings, The Doctor's Book of Home Remedies for Dogs and Cats (PA: Rodale Press 1996): 228*

[13] *Information and tips on stings and bites from personal experiences - J. Lindley.*

3. VETERINARIAN VISITS

If you don't already have a veterinarian, choose one wisely. Remember, as cats get older they may develop more health problems. Do not choose a veterinarian because you like him, or her. Choose the one your cat seems to be the most comfortable with, -she's the patient. If the patient likes her doctor, visits will be easier for all concerned. Some older cats 'stress-out' badly going to the veterinarian. The stress can be worse than what's actually ailing her. If visits cause severe stress to your cat you should phone your veterinarian first. Many problems can be handled over the phone with advice given. Between the ages of 12 to 14 years, your cat should be pretty emotionally stable, so, this is a good time to take her to the veterinarian. Also 16 years is another fairly stable age, good time for a complete physical. It is important to remember to keep alert for signs of trouble, particularly hyperthyroidism and diabetes mellitus symptoms.

ROUTINE EXAM

A routine examination of your older cat should include the following:

1. A quick review of her file;
2. Check weight and temperature;
3. Check eyes, ears, nose, mouth, gums, teeth, and throat;
4. Feeling for any body swellings, and lumps;
5. Listening to her heart;
6. Evaluation of her body weight and muscle mass;
7. Discussion of diet;
8. If anything looks unusual your veterinarian may suggest a blood panel be run to check for endocrine secretion levels, or testing for feline leukemia virus, feline aids, and other potentially critical disease.

This is also a good time for you to ask any questions you might have regarding your cat's health, both present and future.

VACCINATIONS AND BOOSTERS AND TESTS

Years ago it was 'give your cat one initial vaccination, followed by one booster 2 weeks later, and your cat was protected for her life'. Nowadays things are quite different. Not only are cats living longer but, they are also at more risk of contact with unvaccinated cats. The American Veterinary Medical Association recommends boosters to be given annually. My, personal, recommendation is yearly boosters for the first ten years. After that, boosters every other year should be sufficient, especially if your cat is a single house cat. If you plan to travel and will be boarding your cat, you should speak to your veterinarian about an extra booster shot to protect her, while she's in close contact with other cats. Most boarding kennels require testing for feline leukemia virus and feline aids before you bring your cat in. This protects their other cats, should your cat be a carrier of these diseases. After you return and have brought your cat home, you may want to have her retested in about one month, to make sure she didn't pick up anything while she was boarded. Remember 'an ounce of prevention is worth a pound of cure'

SURGERY AND ANESTHESIA

Years ago any surgery was quite a risk for an older cat, even spay and neuter surgery. Today, the risks are minimized, even for cats in their late teens and twenties. Now we must deal with the individual cat, i.e. what their physical condition is prior to surgery. If your cat is very debilitated, i.e. thin or dehydrated, she will need vitamin therapy and plenty of fluids to prepare her prior to her surgery. On very old cats a blood panel will be run before surgery, to help the veterinarian determine internal organ condition.

Surgery, on the older cat, should be limited to: the correction of physiological dysfunction, as in heart disease, thyroid disease and kidney disease; removal of diseased or unwanted new growths, such as tumors, that interfere with normal functions; and any necessary emergency surgery, needed to maintain the life of your cat.[1] Sometimes an older cat will require oral surgery, for dentistry, i.e. teeth extractions and cleaning. This would not be necessarily considered as a surgery but your veterinarian may need to utilize an anesthetic to perform it.

Anesthesia risks used to be the greatest fear for concerned cat owners, myself included. This fear was due, mostly, to the length of time the anesthetic took to wear off, or metabolize. Many older cats were just too weak to last it out. Nowadays, anesthetics are much quicker to metabolize and the older cats have very little after effects. There is, currently, quite a selection of anesthetics available for your veterinarian to use. In fairly simple procedures there are tranquilizers, or sedatives, to be used with a local anesthetic. General anesthesia is used because the cat, in most cases, will not hold still long enough to do what may be required. In regards to kidney problems, or urinary blockage, where a male cat needs catheterization (a urethral catheter inserted), some will actually hold still, others are so traumatized that they require a general anesthetic given. General anesthetics can be given via injection, for short term procedures, inhalation (gas), for longer ones, or a combination of both. Safety and good recovery are the prime factors in choosing the anesthetic for your cat. Your veterinarian will choose one that is the safest for your cat's heart, lungs and kidneys.

During surgery, your cat will be monitored for pulse rate and strength, respirations and gum color. In some cases blood pressure and urine output will also be monitored. And, of course, the older your cat is the more closely she'll be watched for possible age-related complications.

Recovery time, immediately following surgery, depends on the type of surgery performed as well as the impact of it on your cat. Your veterinarian may want to keep her a few days just for observation. If this is the case please ask about visiting your cat. The separation anxiety can be great if she is closely bonded with you. I have seen some cats die apparently because they thought they were forgotten.

When it's time to bring her home, you may wish to confine her to a room where she will be kept warm and quiet. Your veterinarian may want you to keep notes on her appetite, urine output, water intake, and anything else that looks unusual. If there is an incision you should watch for redness, discharge and any swelling. Don't expect her to be her normal self right away. Remember, recovery time is expected to be at least 24 hours longer for every year over five years of age.[2] Give her plenty of rest time, vitamins (if necessary) and your loving attention and she'll come around as soon as possible.

Weigh carefully the advantages and disadvantages of surgery, on your older cat, but don't put it off because you fear it. Talk to your veterinarian. Surgery, if needed and done timely, can greatly increase the time you can still share, with your cat.

VETERINARIAN VISITS NOTES

[1] *Personal opinion - J. Lindley.*

[2] *Michael S. Bodri, Care of Older Animals, Animal Science, (Scranton, PA: ICS 1994): 43.*

4. PAIN, PAIN MANAGEMENT, TERMINAL ILLNESSES AND ALTERNATIVE REMEDIES

There are some diseases, common to older cats, where surgery is not an option. These are on-going, or chronic, diseases such as heart-, kidney-, liver disease, arthritis and types of cancer. Some of these problems will respond to a regimented special diet. In most cases this is not a cure but a control, to slow down the rate of degeneration. Even with the more serious disorders, it is hard to determine the amount of pain felt by your cat. Her behavior may be your only clue as to how she's feeling. If she sleeps a lot and whines when you move her, you can be pretty sure she's in some discomfort.

Depending on her disorder, your veterinarian may be able to prescribe pain relievers. NEVER give your cat acetaminophen (Tylenol), ibuprofen (Motrin) or naproxen (Alleve), since they cannot be metabolized and can be fatal. Aspirin can be given in small doses, under veterinarian's care.[1] Your veterinarian may also prescribe opioids, opium derivative drugs, for chronic pain in cats.[2] Other medications, more normally, given are corticosteroids, such as prednisone.[3] There are some side effects with long term use of steroids so your veterinarian may base his decision on the age of your cat, as well as her immediate condition. Your veterinarian may also suggest the use of ice packs or heating pads. It's best to leave the pain reliever decisions to a qualified veterinarian.

Sometimes a certain amount of pain is good. In the case of arthritis, some pain will remind your cat when she needs to slow down. Some days will be better than others. On those off-days give her more attention, and call your veterinarian when you need help, that's what they're there for. It is important to keep notes, even on a daily basis, as to how your cat is responding to treatment. These notes can be valuable in making future decisions, both by you and your veterinarian.

ALTERNATIVE REMEDIES

When all else seems to fail, don't lose hope, - there are still 'alternatives'. Alternative medicine, sometimes known as holistic medicine, uses the philosophy that the body will heal itself, if given the proper conditions. These conditions may include; vitamin therapy, massage, chiropractic care, acupuncture, herbal and homeopathic remedies. These are therapies, and remedies, not officially sanctioned by the American Veterinary Medical Association, that may or may not work for your cat. But, when the situation has become an 'anything that will work' one, what's the harm in trying. Your veterinarian may be willing to help you find alternative treatments as well as cooperating with the specialists in each particular field. Many veterinarians get involved because they care about their patient, and you the client. In the case of an older cat, whose body is degenerating with age, many of these remedies will not cure the ailment, but they will alleviate the pain and increase your cat's time with you. I believe as long as my cats are willing to try, so must I.

The following information is for reference and education only. It is not intended to be a substitute for professional advice. It is only intended to show you, the reader, that there may still be hope after normal traditional medicine fails. Please seek advice of appropriate contacts in their specialized field. A list is provided following the information text.

VITAMIN THERAPY and SUPPLEMENTS

For many years the vitamins C and E have been found to be very beneficial to cats. Years ago, before feline leukemia vaccines were developed; people were giving mega doses of vitamin C and E to protect their cats. Other vitamins were also used.

Vitamin C (ascorbic acid) is sometimes given when the cat has a severe infection, or in the case of a debilitated cat. Normally, the cat's body synthesizes vitamin C from glucose,[4] but severe infections sometimes deter this ability. Vitamin C is also given as a urine acidifier. Since vitamin C is water soluble and washes right through the system it may also aid in cleaning the blood.[5]

Vitamin E has been long noted for its healing abilities. It also helps to maintain the structure of muscle cells.[6] This would be beneficial in kidney disease where muscle mass is compromised.

Vitamin Bl (thiamine) B2 (riboflavin) and B6 (pyridoxine) are all important for protein metabolism, energy. They also are used (in NutriCal®) to stimulate appetite in a debilitated cat.

NutriCal® is an excellent source of vitamin supplementation for older cats. It comes in a tube and your cat can lick a little off your finger each day. Remember it is a supplement and is not sufficient to maintain the cat. It is available through most veterinarians as well as feed stores, pet supply outlets and pet shops. It is inexpensive and worth every cent.

For a cat with kidney disease you might try feeding her baby food. It's full of vitamins and easy for the kidneys to process. I've found that the veal baby food may be too rich but the chicken and turkey ones work well.

CHIROPRACTIC THERAPY

This was pretty much discussed in Chapter II Dem Bones. Chiropractics concentrate on bone manipulation with emphasis on the spinal vertebrae. If your cat is extremely arthritic it is my advice that you take her to a chiropractor to make sure everything is in proper alignment. There should be no pinched nerves or stretched muscles, to add to her arthritic pain. If her back is in proper alignment it should also relieve any undue pressure on her lower joints, i.e. elbows and ankles.[7]

ACUPUNCTURE

Acupuncture can be used in conjunction with chiropractics, as well as herbal and homeopathic remedies. It is the use of needles, strategically placed, to relieve pain.

It is an ancient practice originating in China more than 3,000 years ago.[8] The needles are inserted in acupoints, lying just below the skin. This stimulates the nerves and can increase circulation, relieve muscle spasms and release hormones, such as cortisol, to control pain.[9] Acupuncture can help conditions, in cats, such as paralysis, arthritis, allergies, asthma, diarrhea, constipation and respiratory and skin problems.[10]

HERBS AND HOMEOPATHY

The origin of herbs has been lost in antiquity. Animals have been doing it instinctively since forever. The first prehistoric man to injure himself and reach for a leaf to cover it was using the art of herbal medicine. Many of the herbal formulas, used in China, were written nearly 1800 years ago and are still used today.[11] The earliest written herbal records were discovered in Egypt (Ebers Papyrus c. 1500 BC) and Assyria (65OBC).[12]

The main premise with herbal medicine is to promote maintenance of good health through the reinforcement of the body's own natural defenses.[13] Similarly, homeopathy is the use of like to cure like, with the good health provided by the body's defense system. Homeopathy came about 200 years ago with the studies of its originator, Samuel Hahnemann, but is based on the beliefs of Hippocrates and Paracelsus.[14] Both therapies are achieved through the use of herbs. The main difference is what herb and its preparation. Herbal medicine takes the whole herb, utilizing leaves, stems, flowers and sometimes roots in its concoctions.[15] Homeopathy takes an herb that will produce the same symptoms as the ailment, extracts the oil, or juice, of the herb and minimizes it to a micro amount for use as a lotion, liquid, sugar pill, or tablet.[16] Hopefully the end result of both therapies is the same - normal good health. Herbal remedies, and now some homeopathic remedies, may be purchased from Health Food Stores, but many homeopathic remedies must still be administered by a practitioner.

When referring to the following chart, remember some of these may work, some won't and there's a slim chance of a reaction. In most cases it would be wise to consult a specialist for their opinion as well as other possible remedies. A list of specialists and practitioners follows the chart.

I WOULD LIKE TO REMIND YOU THAT CATS ARE NOT SMALL PEOPLE, OR SMALL DOGS IN THEIR BASIC METABOLISM. YOU MAY WISH TO CONSULT WITH YOUR VETERINARIAN PRIOR TO USING ANY OF THE FOLLOWING REMEDIES.

ALTERNATIVE REMEDIES

Ailment		Suggestive Treatment
1. HYPERTHYROIDISM Including associated Heart Disease (enlarged and over active heart) Congestive Heart Disease	Herbal R:	Garlic (lowers blood pressure) Hawthorn berries (slows over rapid heart beat and diminishes blood pressure) Blessed Thistle (strengthens heart w/ muscle)
2. KIDNEY/BLADDER DISEASE	Homeo R:	Kidney – Aconite 30 and Arsenicum Alb 30 Bladder-Apis 3x (infreq. urin.) Cantharis 3 (bloody or painful urination)
	Herbal R:	Agrimony/Bearberry/Couch Grass/ Pyssissewa
w/Hypertension		Garlic – to lower blood pressure
3. LIVER DISEASE	Vitamins:	C and E to promote cell activity and healing
	Homeo R:	Jaundice-Chelidonium Maj 6 w/Bryonia 6, after recovery sulphur 30
	Herbal R:	Agrimony/Aloe*/Bindweed/Dodder Dandelion/Milk and Blessed Thistles
4. BREATHING PROBLEMS Asthma, colds, allergies, nasal discharge and Bronchitis	Homeo R:	Asthma – Sulphur 30/Arsenicum Alb 30/Bryonia 6 (frothy) Spongia ix (panting) Bronchitis – Aconite 30 Rhus Tox 6/Bryonia 6 Nasal Dis. – Pulsatilla 30 Silicea 30 or Psorinum 200
	Herbal R:	Agrimony/Elecampane/Garlic/ Mullenin/Seneca/Snakeroot

*Aloe – valued as a tonic, purgative and jaundice remedy regenerates damaged tissues.

Ailment		**Suggestive Treatment**
5. ARTHRITIS/RHEUMATISM	Chiropractic:	visit/Acupuncture
	Homeo R:	Rhus Tox 30 alternated w/Bryonia Alb 30
	Herbal R:	Chaparral/German and Roman Chamomile/Meadowsweet/Mormon Tea
	Home R:	heating pad
6. DIARRHEA	Homeo R:	Pulsatilia 6 and Arsenicum Alb 3
	Herbal R:	Agtimony/Canaigre Root/Cranesbill
	Home R:	Cottage Cheese/Cheese
7. CONSTIPATION	Homeo R:	Nux Vomica 6/Bryonia 6 and Opium 3
	Herbal R:	Aloe*/Bindweed/Bitter Dock Dodder/Buckthorn
	Home R:	Petroleum jelly or Butter Sometimes milk will help
8. GUMS AND TEETH	Vitamins:	C and E
9. CANCERS	Homeo R:	Phytolacca 30 (mammary tumors)
	Herbal R:	Chaparral
10. DIABETES	Herbal R:	ONION studies indicate that it reduces hypertension and high blood sugar

* Aloe – valued as a tonic, purgative and jaundice remedy regenerates damaged tissues.

CHART INFORMATION

Based from:
Reader's Digest magic and medicines of plants, Reader's Digest; 1986
Treatment of Cats by Homepathy, K. Shepherd, 1960 reprinted 1984 Hillman
Printers Ltd. Frome, England.

List of Specialists/Practitioners

1. American Holistic Veterinary Medical Association
   2214 Old Emmorton Rd.
   Bel Air, MD 21015

2. American Veterinary Chiropractic Assoc.
   P.O. Box 249
   Port Byron, IL

3. Association of Natural Medicine Pharmacists
   Champs de Elysses
   Forestville, CA 95436

4. International Veterinary Acupuncture Society
   2140 Conestoga Rd
   Chester Springs, PA 19425

5. National Center for Homeopathy
   801 N. Fairfax St., Ste. 306
   Alexandria, VA 22314

Listings from: Case for Alternative Health Care, by Marion Lane,
1996, January, Cat Fancy, pg. 39. (some of these may have changed)

Judith Lindley

NOTES

1 *W. Bradford Swift, "Coping With Pain", Cats Magazine (March 1996): 33.*

2 *ibid.*

3 *ibid.*

4 *June Kirvan-Tuttle and Mark L. Morris Jr., Feline Nutritional Requirements, The Cornell Book of Cats, (N.Y.:*
   Villard Books d. Random House 1992): 77.

5 *Personal observations - J. Lindley.*

6 *June Kirvan-Tuttle and Mark L. Morris Jr., Feline Nutritional Requirements, The Cornell Book of Cats (N.Y.: Villard Books d. Random House 1992): 76.*

7 *Personal opinion - J. Lindley.*

8 *Marion Lane, "The Case for Alternative Health Care", Cat Fancy Magazine (Jan. 1996): 38.*

9 *ibid: pg 40.*

10 *Marion Lane, "The Case for Alternative Health Care" Cat Fancy Magazine (Jan 1996): 40.*

11 *Joelle Steele, "What is Holistic Health Care?", I Love Cats Mag. (May/June 1994): 48.*

12 *F. Fletcher Hyde, Herbal Medicine, A Visual Encyclopedia of Unconventional Medicine (N.Y.: Crown Pub, 1979): 116.*

13 *Joelle Steele, "What is Holistic Health Care?", I Love Cats magazine (May/June 1994): 48.*

14 *Homeopathy, A Visual Encyclopedia of Unconventional Medicine (N.Y.: Crown Pub. 1979): 22.*

15 *Herbal Medicine, A Visual Encyclopedia of Unconventional Medicine (N.Y.: Crown Pub. 1979): 116.*

16 *Cecil Craig, (1974) Homeopathy: What it is, How it works, (L.A., CA: Standard Homeopathic Co., 1988): pamphlet.*

THE LAST MEOW

The last few years of your cat's life, starting from fifteen years old, perhaps as early as fourteen years, you will be making many adjustments. These adjustments will start out slow at first, so slow that you may hardly notice you're making them. The first changes I made were in environmental temperature. If your house is thermostatically controlled you will need to adjust the thermostat slightly warmer in the winter and slightly cooler in the summer. Your older cat may have a difficult time regulating her body temperature. You should also, if you haven't already, develop a regular feeding routine with your cat. It's easier for her to be fed at regular times in the same location, that way she'll know what to expect. If your cat is going deaf, it may come on so slowly that you may not notice it at first. If you feed her at regular times she'll show up without being called and unless you call her, directly, you may never realize she's deaf. If she's a single household cat make sure she sees you, then try clapping or use hand signals. Touch her often, but from the front when she sees you. Deaf cats can be easily startled which may cause undue stress. If she's blind, touch, again, is important. Make lots of happy noises to let her know she's not alone. Don't move the furniture around or she'll become confused.

The hardest adjustment you will make is when her end comes near. We all must realize that death is inevitable and no matter what we do we can't put it off forever, but we can love them while we have them. If your cat is in pain, and suffering with a terminal illness, you may have to make the difficult decision of euthanasia. We'd all like to see our beloved companions just pass away in their sleep but sometimes we don't have that option.

Whether your cat passes away or you pass on first, there's always one left behind to grieve. There are lots of books available on grief, so I'll just touch on this subject. Grieving is a very natural response and it must be felt before healing can begin and the one left behind can continue on. Do not rush the grieving process, it affects each of us differently, cats included. It is a very personal feeling. Try to remember the happy times - your cat would want it that way.

1. THAT DIFFICULT CHOICE - EUTHANASIA

If your cat is terminally ill and diagnosed as such, you may need to determine if she is suffering. Often, cats bear their pain extremely well and are just happy to be around you until their last breath. If she appears to be in great pain you may wish to consider euthanasia to end her suffering. It is a very difficult choice to make. Before you make the decision, ask yourself a few questions: Does the pain outweigh the pleasure in her life? Can I continue to provide her with the required care? and, Am I stealing what's left of her life or relieving her pain? Please try not to let money enter into your decision to terminate her life, you may regret it later. Your veterinarian should be able to help you evaluate your cat's degree of suffering, which will aid in your decision.

Euthanasia is derived from Greek eu (good) and thanatos (death) and means the act of causing death painlessly.[1] Most veterinarians inject a large over dose of a barbiturate, which depresses the nervous system. The drug enters the bloodstream and the cat goes to sleep usually within 3 seconds, the feeling of pain ceases and the heart ceases to function, death arrives peacefully within a minute or less. I usually prefer to be with my animals up to their last breath, holding them. If you do not feel up to it, I'm sure your veterinarian will understand. Some cats are in so much pain that they block everything around themselves out, so she might not even realize you're there with her.

The trouble with today's society, in relation to cats, is sometimes they are considered to be disposable animals. The Animal Control Shelters euthanize one after the other, regardless of age or health; they say it's due to the overwhelming numbers. Some people take their older cats to these Shelters, because they can't deal with advancing age and death of their cat. If your cat has been with you a long time, and she becomes terminally ill she will rely on you to care for her enough to make the necessary decisions even when it comes to terminating her life.

2. GRIEVING

The most important thing you need to know, about grief, is that it is a perfectly natural process. I believe that we grieve in proportion to the degree we loved. My grandmother passed on when I was seventeen years old and I grieved her loss. Strangely, I grieved more for my cat, Grayless (she was 18½ yrs.), and I was 38 years old then. I felt guilty about the different degree of grief for many years, until I finally realized that Grayless was more a part of my life than my grandmother was. I only saw my grandmother once in awhile and Grayless was with me most of the time.

Besides the degree, or depth, of grief there are different stages of grief. In addition to the expected depression, you may feel guilty (particularly if euthanasia was involved) denial, anger and you may go through a sort of bargaining process. Denial, usually, wears off as reality of death sets in. Bargaining is when you torture yourself, as in 'if I had taken better care of her, this wouldn't have happened'. To deal with this phase, you need to be fatalistic. All creatures are born and will die in God's time. In other words, she would have died no matter what you did, if it was her time. Accept the fact that if it wasn't her time to go, God wouldn't have taken her. Even in the case of euthanization, do not feel guilty; you would not have been placed in that situation unless it was deemed necessary and God would not have wished your cat to suffer needlessly. Anger is what we, personally and selfishly, feel for our own loss. You need to feel these things before you can move on.

Sometimes I get angry because I love too deeply and the loss makes me feel empty and hurt. I let the love I shared with my cats slowly fill the hole and the anger subsides to good memories. Grief is a very personal thing, you may have some, or all, of these emotions, but whatever you feel know that it does take time to heal - but someday you will heal.

There are others who may grieve the loss of your cat. If you have family, especially younger children, they may also go through the grieving process, each in their own depth, according to their closeness to your deceased cat. Your children may want to know what happens to your cat now. I've always told my children that God has a place in Heaven for our pets, as well as humans. I truly believe that the soul is the spark of life, which resides in us all, and, if that life is full of love there definitely is a place in Heaven for all of us, humans and their animal companions. Besides that, if cats aren't allowed in Heaven, I'm not sure I want to go there either. I cannot imagine not having animals around,-any place.

Other members of your family household may also grieve the loss of a friend. If you have other companion cats, they will need to be watched closely for signs of grief, such as refusing to eat and general moping. They, too, will need extra comforting by you. Even dogs have been known to grieve for a companion cat. I have seen cases of cats, and dogs, willing themselves to death because they have lost their companions.

Do not rush out and try to replace your cat. Each cat is as individual as each human is and cannot be replaced, but can be remembered. When you begin to heal your emptiness and sadness will be replaced with loving memories, and after all isn't that how your cat would want to be remembered.

Following the death of my cat, Grayless, I wrote:

"Memories are filled with love, especially when they're filled with your cat". I am glad I was able to share her life with her, and I'm able to love all the more for knowing her. Appreciate what your cat was able to give you, and love her memory in tribute to her life.

> TO LIKE A CAT, IS TO LET HER INTO YOUR LIFE,
>
> TO LOVE A CAT, IS TO LET HER INTO YOUR HEART,
>
> TO BE LOVED BY YOUR CAT, IS TO ALLOW HER TO GIVE HER
>
> ONE SPECIAL GIFT - UNCONDITIONAL LOVE.
>
> -JUDITH LINDLEY

NOTE

[1] *Euthanasia, Webster's New World Dictionary, Warner Books Paperback Edition, (N.Y.: Warner Books, 1990): 205.*

CHAPTER VI. SOMETHING ABOUT ALBERT

In 1987, one of my older cats was featured on local news and then national network news. He wasn't particularly unusual, just a large gray tiger with bright blue eyes and a loving purr-sonality. Being rather large nearly 18 pounds, and positioning himself pretty squarely in the midst of things so he could soak up as much attention as possible, is probably why the newscaster was drawn to pick him up. Stunned by his weight she chose to support him on a perch while she discussed our rescue unit's foster feline adoption program.

Albert came to me from very humble surroundings. Surroundings, chosen rather than beginnings, because he just arrived in the neighborhood, of two elderly ladies, one day. Already a neutered adult Albert was most likely 'dumped' because his people had outgrown their fondness for him.

I originally encountered Albert when I visited my lady friend one morning for coffee, the summer of 1985. To my best judgment, prior to a closer examination of teeth, Albert appeared to be about 8 years (plus or minus) old. He moved around the yard with a confident poise and escorted the youngest feline guests. He was a big boned cat, a little on the lean side, slightly dull coat, a few scars here and there, with gray tiger stripes and bright blue eyes, which spoke of Siamese ancestry. He looked to be about 14 pounds, which was still too thin for his big bone structure. What I first noticed was how friendly he was. No matter what he was doing, the minute I stepped into the yard there he was, rubbing against my leg. And, of course, if he didn't get a pet immediately he'd hump up in the air and rub higher, then drop and circle in front of me, meowing until I'd stoop to pet him or scratch his ears. Then, he'd wind about my legs while I attempted to get to the front door. He was a most affectionate stray.

Albert officially came to live with me January of 1987. He had been having some difficulties with a younger tom and his lady worried about his well-being. Fighting among outside males is usually for dominance and if the younger one wins the older one may be run off, or at least seriously injured. After a few boisterous scraps his lady thought it best to call me.

Having been an outside cat, for a number of years, Albert adjusted to his cattery life pretty well. When he first arrived there were approximately sixty cats in the colony. Albert chose to stay on the inside shelves watching, more or less, from an owl's point of view. Upon arrival Albert weighed in at 14½ pounds. That was not bad for a stray. His coat was no longer dull, but had a nice glossy sheen to it. On closer examination of his teeth, there was one deep grain line and one partial grain line on his right and left fangs (canine teeth). This placed him between 10 and 12 years old. He was exceptionally healthy for being that old! There were other signs of advancing age, flecks in the eye iris, more use of entire paws and a lot of basking in the sun.

In our colony there is no particular dominant male or female, but if you had to choose one it would have been Albert. Whether he peered down from the shelf or from the couch-bed he definitely was an impressive gentle-cat. He lorded over everyone with a quiet regal manner. His nicknames alternated from "Fat Albert" to "Prince Albert". And, everyone loved him. His own feline companions and human visitors equally adored him.

Albert had about 3 sick days during his stay with me. I have never really felt that one owns a cat. Cats are very much individuals and entirely in charge of themselves, but they do enjoy our companionship and attention and will graciously share our love. One nice thing about cats, and most domestic animals, is that they love you for yourself, not because you have money or position, and about the most they ask in return is a comfortable place to rest and decent food. Of course the occasional pat is definitely a must. Albert was so secure in his relationships that when he was in trouble he simply waited for me to pick him up and take him to the vet. He knew I would help him, so he behaved like the purr-fect gentle cat he was. He never even gave the vet trouble as he checked for urinary obstruction. Albert had been straining to urinate and, with his Siamese heredity indicating possible small ducts inside, he had exhibited all the classic symptoms of feline urological syndrome, or urinary blockage. Fortunately the vet was able to force out the urine by a gentle massage and prescribed some small pills. Under normal circumstances I'm sure a special diet would have been indicated but Albert was already enjoying dry Iams, which is low in ash. This sick period lasted only about 2 days, in 1989. Albert was very resilient. He never let anything get him down for long, especially if it caused any problems with his eating. He now tipped the scales at nearly 18 pounds, and looked extremely fit for a 14 year old. He remained in excellent health through summer of 1994, when he would have been somewhere around 18 years old.

As everything gets older, there are more noticeable changes first in actions then in overall appearance. Albert had finally begun to slow down. He dropped in weight to 15 pounds and was no longer on the shelves, preferring the couch-bed or a sunny area outside. In early November he had a very slight eye discharge, the first indication of sinus breakdown. Around November 20th he developed a slight nose sniffle. Less active now and choosing to quietly watch the others from his corner of the couch-bed, he was still respected by everyone. The nurse cat on duty was a brown tiger longhair named Greycat. Greycat washed Albert's face and ears on a twice a day basis, and rested continuously by his side. November 24, 1994, early morning, Albert passed away. His nurse cat was still by his side when I came in. Albert was buried, with prayers and full honors as due his status, on Paw Hill, behind our cattery, where his spirit can continue to watch over those he loved. We all miss him but he lived and died with a great dignity and the grace that befits an older cat.

Photo by J. Lindley

Our grand old Albert, surely a Prince among purrers.

CONCLUSION

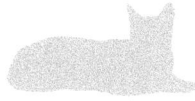

It's been over 25 years since I put pen to paper and wrote On Older Cats. It's amazing how little I had to change to update the information for this second edition. Of course there have been many advancements in veterinary science but not too many changes with respect to the over all care of our beloved feline companions. Their senses and body systems still function the same way, available diets, on the market, have changed as the cat food companies do more research and there are a multitude of cat beds and activity toys specifically geared for the older cat.

I've tried to smooth out the rough spots in On Older Cats, first edition, and have changed some of the drawings for easier reading. You will also find new photos. My daughter, Pamela Adams and her friend Jaime Rea, cropped, enhanced and set the photos. I wish to thank all the wonderful people who sent in the photos of their beautiful cats. I'm truly honored to have them to display.

Lastly, although I am not a veterinarian, I've had over 50 years of hands on experience and I may have seen things they haven't. However, all the experience is no good unless you share it. So, please read this, enjoy it and keep it for future reference. Remember, if you notice anything unusual with your older cat please see a veterinarian. Give your cat a good diet, plenty of fresh water, a good happy environment and lots of attention and love and you will have many enjoyable years to share together.

SUGGESTED READINGS

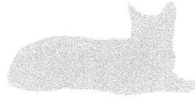

Over the years there have been many articles written, with regards to aging animals. These are the best articles on aging cats, I've come across:

1. "How Old is Old?" by Ian Dunbar, DVM. April 1991, Cat Fancy Magazine, pgs. 14-20.
2. "Senior Cats" by K.E. Segnar. April 1991, Cat Fancy Magazine, pgs. 42-51.
3. "Aging Gracefully" by Kim Campbell Thornton, October 1994, Cat Fancy Magazine, pgs. 36-40.
4. "The Older Cat", Catnip, Tufts Univ. Newsletter, August 1994, pgs. 4-6.

There are a great number of books about cats available, but I think the most complete book is: Cornell's Book of Cats, by Faculty, Staff and Associates, The Cornell Feline Health Center, College of Veterinary Medicine, Edited by Mordecai Siegal, (N.Y. Villard Books d. Random House 1992) and their Second Edition (1997).

BIBLIOGRAPHY

Anderson, Robert and Barbara Wrede. Digestive System, Caring For Older Dogs and Cats. Charlotte,Vt: Williamson Pub. Co. 1990: 33-38.

Barlough, Jeffrey E. Immune System and Disorders, The Cornell Book of Cats. New York: Villard Books, a div. of Random House, 1992: 249-253.

Barlough, Jeffrey E. Musculoskeletal System and Disorders, The Cornell Book of Cats. New York: Villard Books, a div. of Random House, 1992: 199-205.

Barlough, Jeffrey E., June Kirvan-Tuttle and Leo A. Wuori. Endocrine System and Metabolic Disorders, The Cornell Book of Cats. New York: Villard Books, a div. of Random House, 1992: 243-248.

Barlough, Jeffrey E., Linda Susan Jorgensen and Ronald C. Riis. Sensory Organs and Disorders, The Cornell Book of Cats. New York: Villard Books, a div. of Random House, 1992: 162-176.

Christensen, Wendy. "The Wondrous Whiskers", Cat Fancy Magazine, (December 1994): 32-33.

Dengler, Pat. "Do Cats Go To Heaven?", Cat Fancy Magazine, (December 1987): 25-28.

Diamond, Barbara L. "How Cats Purr", Cat Fancy Magazine, (June 1988): 56-59.

Dillman, Lori. "How To Pet A Cat", I Love Cats Magazine, (March/April 1996): 18-21.

Enright, Helen. "Coats and Claws", Cat Fancy Magazine, (April 1991): 22-25.

Enright, Helen. "The Well-Groomed Cat", Cat Fancy Magazine, (October 1991): 22-26.

Goulart, Frances Sheridan. "Massaging Your Cat to Better Health", I Love Cats Magazine, (July/Aug 1993): 22-25.

Helstrom, Bob. "When the Fur Flies", Cats Magazine, (June 1996): 42-45.

Hoskins, Johnny D. and June Kirvan-Tuttle. Urinary System and Disorders, The Cornell Book of Cats. New York: Villard Books a div. of Random House, 1992: 206-211.

Houpt, Katherine A. Feline Behavior and Misbehavior, The Cornell Book of Cats. New York: Villard Books, a div. of Random House, 1992: 51-68.

Kirk, Robert W. and Mordecai Siegal. First Aid and Procedures for Life-Threatening Emergencies, The Cornell Book of Cats. New York: Villard Books, a div. of Random House, 1992: 343-363.

Kirvan-Tuttle, June, Jeffrey E. Barlough, Mordecai Siegal and Leo A. Wuori. Aging Cats and Disorders, The Cornell Book of Cats. New York: Villard Books, a div. of Random House, 1992: 309-314.

Kirvan-Tuttle, June and Mark L. Morris Jr. Feline Nutritional Requirements, The Cornell Book of Cats. New York: Villard Books, a div. of Random House, 1992: 71-78.

Lane, Marion. "The Case for Alternative Health Care", Cat Fancy Magazine, (Jan.1996): 36-43.

Lein, Donald. Reproductive Disorders, The Cornell Book of Cats. New York: Villard Books, a div. of Random House, 1992: 108-115.

Moise, N. Sydney. Circulatory System and Disorders, The Cornell Book of Cats. New York: Villard Books, a div. of Random House, 1992: 187-198.

Morris, Mark L. and June Kirvan-Tuttle. Feeding Cats and Diseases of Dietary Origin, The Cornell Book of Cats. New York: Villard Books, a div. of Random House, 1992: 79-90.

Morrisey, Thomas G. "Catanatomy", Cornell's Feline Health Center's Perspectives On Cats, (Summer 1990): 3-5.

Muller, George H., Robert W. Kirk and Danny W. Scott. Lentigo Simplex in Orange Cats, Small Animal Dermatology 4th Ed. Philadelphia: W.B. Saunders Co. 1989: 707-708.

Nelson, Wendy L. "When Your Best Friend Dies", Cat Fancy Magazine, (March 1992): 36-39.

Pavia, Audry. "Cross Country Cats", Cat Fancy Magazine, (July 1994): 12-19.

Peiffer, Robert L. Jr. Small Animal Opthalmology. Philadelphia: W.B. Saunders Co. 1989: 185-187.

Phillips, Bill and Debbie. "In Awe of the Paw", Cat Fancy Magazine, (March 1994): 32-39.

Pollock, Roy V.H.. Digestive System and Disorders, The Cornell Book of Cats. New York: Villard Books, a div. of Random House, 1992: 226-237.

Salzberg, Kathy. "Scratching Out the Truth on Paws and Claws", Cat Fancy Magazine, (Feb. 1995): 50-55.

Scott, Danny W. Skin and Disorders, The Cornell Book of Cats. New York: Villard Books, a div. of Random House, 1992: 143-161.

Scott, Fred W. The Respiratory System and Disorders, The Cornell Book of Cats. New York: Villard Books, a div. of Random House, 1992: 218-225.

Shojai, Amy.D. "The Food of Life", Cat Fancy Magazine, (May 1995): 34-39.

Shojai, Amy D. "The Sensitive Nose", Cat Fancy Magazine, (May 1994): 20-24.

Steele, Joelle. "What Is Holistic Health Care?", I Love Cats Magazine, (May/June 1994): 46-48.

Summers, Brian A. and Jeffrey E. Barlough. Nervous System and Disorders, The Cornell Book of Cats. New York: Villard Books, a div. of Random House, 1992: 212-217.

Swift, W. Bradford. "Coping With Pain", Cats Magazine, (March 1996): 30-33.

Tuttle, June E. "Feline Bronchial Diseases", Cornell's Perspectives On Cats, (Summer 1990): 1-2.

Weatherford, Cora. "Breaking Bad Cat Behavior", I Love Cats Magazine, (March/April 1996): 61-63.

Wilbourn, Carol C. Cat Talk, What Your Cat Is Trying To Tell You. New York: MacMillan Pub. Co. 1979: 33-42, 46-68 and 94-107.

Wuori, Leo A. Surgery and Postoperative Care, The Cornell Book of Cats. New York: Villard Books, a div. of Random House, 1992: 326-334.

"Anesthesia", Catnip, a Newsletter from Tufts University School of Veterinary Medicine, (Vol. 1, No. 3, 1993): 1-3.

"Fabulous Fur", Catnip, a Newsletter from Tufts University School of Veterinary Medicine, (Oct. 1994): 1-3.

"Feline Diabetes", Catnip, a Newsletter from Tufts University School of Veterinary Medicine, (July 1994): 4-6.

"Feline First Aid", Catnip, a Newsletter from Tufts University School of Veterinary Medicine, (Dec. 1995): 1-3.

"From the Heart", Catnip, a Newsletter from Tufts University School of Veterinary Medicine, (Jan. 1995): 4-6.

"Litterbox Problem?...", Cornell's Animal Health Newsletter, (March. 1996): 1-2.

"Owners Guide to Giving A Home Health Exam", Cornell's Perspectives On Cats, (Winter 1991): 1-2.

"Pain Management", Catnip, a Newsletter from Tufts University School of Veterinary Medicine, (Aug. 1994): 1-3.

"Saying Goodbye", Catnip, a Newsletter from Tufts University School of Veterinary Medicine, (Sept. 1995): 4-6.

"The Filtering Station of the Body", Catnip, a Newsletter from Tufts University School of Veterinary Medicine, (Sept. 1995): 1-3.

"The River of Life", Catnip, a Newsletter from Tufts University School of Veterinary Medicine, (Jan. 1994): 1-3.

"Wonderful Whiskers", Catnip, a Newsletter from Tufts University School of Veterinary Medicine, (Jan. 1997): 4-5.

Photo by J. Lindley

www.ingramcontent.com/pod-product-compliance
Lightning Source LLC
Chambersburg PA
CBHW080417030426
42335CBC0020B/2487